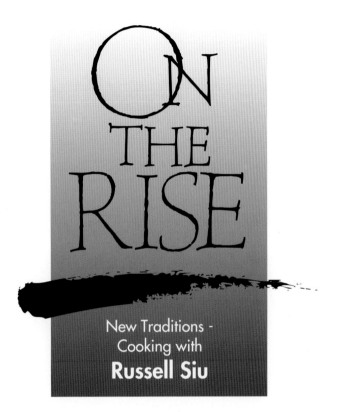

ON THE RISE

New Traditions -
Cooking with
Russell Siu

By -
Russell W.J. Siu

Publisher -
L.A.K. Enterprises
Lisa A. Kim

Photographs by -
Ric Noyle

Text by -
Arnold T. Hiura & James Grant Benton

Food Stylists -
Jim Gillespie
Lisa Siu (*desserts*)
Camille Hendrickson

Book Design by -
Kramer & Associates Design

Printed in Hong Kong

ISBN 0-9654443-0-9

Library of Congress Catalog Card Number: 96-77949
      On the Rise: New Traditions -
      Cooking with Russell Siu
      Russell Siu
      Photography by: Ric Noyle

Art direction: Kramer & Associates Design
Mechanical production: Geo Loyo,
Craig Uchimura and Nicole Seu
Kramer & Associates Design

Distributed in the United States by
Li Rus Enterprises
32 Prospect Street
Honolulu, Hawaii 96813 , U.S.A.

Published by
L.A.K. Enterprises

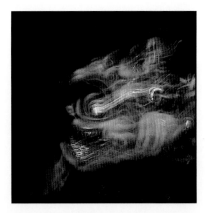

"In any culture, food has the unique power to soothe, uplift and bind people. Cooking offers me an artful means to combine and express the many varied sources of inspiration I have had throughout my life. For the privilege of pursuing such a joyful life's work, I wish to dedicate this book to my parents, Harry and Jessie Siu, for their unwavering love and support."

- Russell W.J. *Siu*

Table of Contents

Introduction

Beginnings

How does one come to see the world? Even the most sophisticated person gains their first glimpse of life through some limited, childhood perspective. My personal odyssey to becoming who I am today began on the streets of Honolulu, Hawaii. . . . Paradise, to most of the world.

Still vivid in my memory are the almost daily treks I would take with my grandfather to Honolulu's bustling Chinatown, where we'd visit the vendors and open-air markets he loved and trusted. Everyday, Grandfather would carefully select the fresh meats, seafood, vegetables and herbs that he would later transform into that evening's meal.

It was quite an adventure for a youngster of 7. The tropical Hawaiian heat rising from the city's sidewalks would slowly baste the aromas of a hundred different things—some commonplace, others you might consider odd or exotic. The cacophony of languages and dialects, as well as the colorful kaleidoscope of complexions and clothing, all added to the rich human stew that was Chinatown. To me it was a comforting place; it was what I was familiar with; it was home.

Grandfather

My Grandfather on my father's side was from China, where they didn't have ice boxes or freezers. What you got that day is what you ate that day, so he always preferred to go to Chinatown every morning to shop for fresh food, selecting a chicken, a spiced duck, vegetables, or a fresh slab of pork.

I can still picture him walking home from the marketplace with a chicken wrapped in newspaper under his arms. He'd kill the chicken, pluck the feathers, and store the giblets in the icebox. Later, he'd steam it, season it, and serve it with rice. Grandfather used to let me help him in the kitchen—plucking the chicken feathers and things like that.

Every night, he'd prepare three or four dishes for dinner—perhaps a meat dish, one fish, one poultry, and one vegetable. Asian-style family dinners differ from a traditional American meal, where you have just one entree. We would always have a variety.

Grandfather was a carpenter by trade. He was good with his hands, and known for his skill in carving Chinese letters. By 4 o'clock each day, however, he would be home, preparing dinner for the nine of us in our household—my grandparents, parents, three sisters, my brother and me. My grandmother and my mother didn't have to cook. The kitchen was grandfather's domain; that's where he did his thing; and that was what he enjoyed the most—cooking.

Grandmother

The situation was very different on my mother's side of the family, where my grandmother did all of the cooking. Because she was born in Hawaii, grandmother was a lot more Americanized. She cooked a variety of foods—from traditional Chinese dishes, to popular local ones, to typical American dishes.

My grandmother was a woman of exceptional taste. We could go to a restaurant, for example, taste something, then ask her, "How do you make this dish?" and she could tell you exactly what was in it. She could go home and recreate the dish again. She was good.

When I was in high school, I practically lived at grandmother's house after school, and then again during the summertime. I liked to watch her cook. I learned a lot from her—things you needed to do to make food look and taste good. I still rely on her tips on how to prepare different types of food. She was especially good at the aesthetics of food presentation. She had a very good eye.

Mother

My mom rarely cooked. Even today, my dad is retired and does all of the cooking. When she did cook, mom would prepare straightforward, "all-American" fare, like pork chops, meat loaf, creamed tuna, fried chicken, baked ham, fresh corned beef and cabbage, roast turkey—things like that.

My mom's thing was baking—she loved to bake. I like to call her "Miss Betty Crocker." I started baking before I started cooking, because of her. We all liked sweets, especially my mom, so I learned to bake from her at a very early age.

These are my beginnings—baking with my mom, helping grandfather at 7 or 8 years of age, then my grandmother when I was about 13 or 14. I grew up enjoying a variety of foods—from Chinese, to traditional American, to the multi-ethnic smorgasbord that we're all exposed to on a daily basis in Hawaii. Later, I learned to combine these influences with a more formal Western training. . . . and, now, all of it comes together in my cooking style.

On the Job Training

I got my first job as a cook when I turned 15. My sister was already working at a local drive-in restaurant. It was pretty simple in those days—they hired girls to work the front counter, and guys to work in the back as cooks. So, when I needed a part-time job, I thought to myself, "Oh, what a great job—look at all the girls . . . ha!" Anyway, I started cooking at the drive-in, learning to make the entire gamut of local dishes, like pork adobo, beef stew, curry stew, chicken hekka, sukiyaki, pork tofu, and other local favorites.

I started at the bottom and worked my way up. I went from cooking at drive-ins, to coffee shops, to restaurants. It gave me an excellent opportunity to learn the whole range of local tastes and cooking styles.

A Turning Point

Later, I attended the University of Hawaii and majored in math and computer science. I didn't plan on becoming a professional chef. Rather, I thought I might become an accountant and, eventually, make a career in the field of finance. When I graduated, I went to apply for an accounting position at a large department store. When I got there, however, the personnel manager told me, "I'm sorry, you don't have the qualifications for the accounting position, but you do have a lot of experience cooking. We'd like to hire you as a cook in our coffee shop." "No. No thank you," I told him "I don't want to cook anymore." I wanted to get away from cooking. After all, I had just completed college. I thought I should at least do something with what I had studied.

Well, that experience served as a turning point for me. At 22, I realized I knew my way around a kitchen pretty well, but I still couldn't call myself a chef. I decided that I wanted to become a real chef. To do that, I knew I needed to go back to college to study cooking, and so I enrolled at Kapiolani Community College.

I continued to learn on my own—tast-

ing, reading and doing my own research. I worked for different chefs at various restaurants, sometimes working two jobs at a time. I even helped people out for free, just so I could learn. My goal was to learn all phases of cooking and food service—from drive-ins and coffee shops, to fine dining, to running banquets. I studied baking and learned to do ice carvings.

The Learning Pyramid

I attacked everything with a passion. When my friend taught me the basics of ice carving, for example, I bought blocks and blocks of ice and practiced on my own. Once, to prepare for an opening on the mainland, my friend and I carved 40 blocks of ice from morning to night.

Basically, I wanted to build a good foundation. I believe in the notion that you need a good base before you can build anything on top of it. Today, I tell my cooks that learning is like a pyramid. A pyramid lasts through the centuries because it has a good foundation. It's built in such a way that nothing can push it over. It's the same with knowledge. Once you build your foundation, you can always do something with it. But if you don't have a sound foundation—knowledge—you're not going to last at anything.

A Hawaiian Journey

There were many exciting developments transforming Hawaii cuisine around this time, and I was very lucky to be a part of it. I entered competitions and won first place for Best New Cook in the Chef's Cuisine competition in 1975. In 1976, I was part of a team that won First Place in a California show, becoming one of the first from Hawaii to be so honored in the culinary arts. I went to Maui in 1978, where I took First Place overall in a competition over there.

Then one day a friend called me up and said, "Hey, Russell, I got a job for you; we go

Big Island." I declined at first, but he made me a good offer, so I went to work for him on the island of Hawaii for three years. After that, I went to Maui, where I worked for a year and then taught at Maui Community College for about a year-and-a-half. Working on the different islands gave me an invaluable opportunity to learn about local people and cultures. On Maui, for example, I stayed with my friend's grandmother, a Native Hawaiian woman who lived near Hana. We used to pick fresh taro to make fresh poi. We used to do a lot of traditional Hawaiian luaus, which we later produced for various hotels. I learned to use native foods and seasonings in my cooking, and learned more about the Hawaiian culture by living on the neighbor islands than I ever could in Honolulu.

In 1979, I returned to Honolulu to work as the executive chef at the Plaza Club, which offered me an excellent opportunity to exercise my creativity and to develop the things I had learned. By this time, my menu had already grown quite diverse. I felt confident enough to try different things and to take a few risks. I enjoyed using fresh local ingredients and preparing them in unique ways, as in dishes like veal, topped with liliko'i sauce, or a lychee almond sauce, or a papaya almond sauce. Other talented local chefs were doing similar things in their own way. In time, something we came to call Hawaii Regional Cuisine was born.

Regional Cuisine

I guess the owners of the Plaza Club liked my work, because in 1982 they appointed me regional chef overseeing the operations of 10 clubs they had in the Dallas-Fort Worth-New Orleans area. At the time, Dallas was still known as a steak-and-potatoes kind of place, but the owners were looking to create something new. When I got there, we decided to feature American cuisine—different regional cuisines from different parts of the United States. We researched hundreds of recipes and then set out to develop our own American cuisine.

I learned to cook Southern-style foods, Cajun foods. Then, over my three years in Texas, I began bringing in food from different parts of the country—like salt-cured country ham made by a farmer in North Carolina and fresh French bread from a bakery in New Orleans. I used to fly fresh fish in from Boston and oysters from Maine. I had hydroponic units growing fresh herbs, and imported fine, grain-fed beef from Chicago.

Later, I began to incorporate Hawaii ingredients into the menu. We did so rather cautiously, since the Dallas club serviced some very well-established individuals in their 60's and older who were pretty set in their ways—they liked their chili with cornbread, steak and potatoes, and they liked their vegetables fully cooked. Slowly, however, we introduced dishes that were a little different, but still seemed familiar to them.

We started by serving fish from Hawaii—like 'opakapaka and mahimahi—because fish is so adaptable. As time went on, we started getting a little more creative, introducing skewers of lobsters, scallops and fish, grilled swordfish steaks. Then I added different kinds of sauces incorporating Hawaiian flavors and ingredients.

I always tried to create something they could relate to, but with a little twist to it. It wasn't way out in left field. The experiment was well received, and the company sent me to Hong Kong to open a club over there. After a year, they promoted me and transferred me to their West Coast Region, where I oversaw operations for 26 clubs. In total, I would spend about nine years in the Northern and Southern California market.

Moving to the West Coast offered me greater latitude to incorporate Asian and Hawaiian influences into my cooking, picking up what I had started at the Plaza Club in Honolulu. California is more of a melting pot, closer to Hawaii in that sense. Northern California, especially the Bay Area, offered me a good opportunity to use the club's resources in creative ways.

My fine dining concepts continued to evolve as I traveled. I did a lot of research, reading and experimenting everywhere I went. I talked to people. I watched. I learned. I developed my taste buds by trying everything.

In 1992, I was ready to return to Hawaii. Today, Euro-Island cuisine has grown in both popularity as well as sophistication, and is really taking off in major markets around the world. I think people like it because they can see it is a healthy style of cooking. It's unique and offers diners very different flavors without too much reliance on heavy sauces. This popularity is reflected in the large number of Asian-themed restaurants opening in major cities across the U.S. continent and Europe, as well as in the popularity of Euro-Asian style restaurants in cities like Tokyo and Hong Kong.

Plain and Simple

All of us who have come to establish ourselves as chefs in Hawaii share some things in common, but we have our own unique styles and identities. I'd characterize my philosophy as being really very plain and simple. I believe in preserving the freshness and naturalness of the food I serve. I don't want sauces to dominate the dish. I want the true flavor of the food to come through. The trick is to make something that already tastes good a little better.

The natural tendency in cooking for fine dining is to want to add 10 ingredients, believing that more is better.

The real challenge, I believe, is to exercise control. When I do sauces, for example, I try not to put too much stuff in them. Our sauces are very subtle; they should enhance—not steal—the flavor of the food they're served with.

My primary market is local, and people in Hawaii value simplicity in taste. At my signature restaurant, 3360 on the Rise, we try to temper our experimentation a bit to meet local tastes. We grew up in these Islands eating a wide variety of Hawaiian and Asian food, so we share some natural preferences in what we eat. We like our food to taste good, of course, and aesthetics are important. We work towards a good presentation. I'm also very conscious about texture, because nobody wants to eat something that's all mushy. Taste, texture and presentation are my three key guiding principles. And, finally, I believe in serving good-sized portions, so customers know they are getting good value for their dollar.

The Creative Process

I enjoy the creative process. Sometimes I create dishes and design menus by myself, while at other times I work with my chefs to put a dish together as a team. In a collaborative situation, I try to get everybody involved. If everyone feels a part of the project, they'll put their heart and soul into preparing it. In the process, I learn from them as they learn from me.

As we're working on something new, I'll ask the others, "Taste the sauce. What do you taste?" I train them to always ask themselves, "Does it taste good?" "Will people like it?" "Does it blow me away?" "Does it create that 'feeling' in you?" If it doesn't, it's not good enough. You've got to keep working at it some more.

Perfect Stew

We're always modifying our dishes, striving to make something good better. Take our lunches at Kakaako Kitchen, for example. Even if we've had beef stew on the menu since we opened, I go in and taste the stew every day. We might look at the way the carrots are cut—maybe they're a little too big; maybe we should blanch them. We work on things like that. Even our popular shoyu chicken recipe was changed more than five times. Even if people already like something, you can make subtle changes to it that will make them think, "Wow. This tastes really good. I can't figure out what's different about it, but it's better."

Evolution

I know my Euro-Island cuisine has its roots firmly anchored deep in my childhood; it has grown and matured as I have. It found formal expression during my tenure at the Plaza Club in Honolulu in the '70s, and was further transformed in the '80s as I worked in various cities across the continental U.S. and in Asia. What began as an exciting experiment got pushed to higher levels as I moved around.

At every level, you have to constantly push yourself to create that special dish. I equate this process to a writer writing a script—you put some words down, then you decide maybe you need a little bit more of this or that, so you change this word, change that word, until you finally come up with a rough draft. After more revisions, you arrive at a script. Even then, the creative process continues throughout the production phases. It continues to evolve. It's the same with food. Cooking is evolution.

-Russell W.J. Siu

I'm sorry, but I have to say that some people just can't cook. They don't have the eye to cook, or they don't have the palate, or lack some combination of the two. One time a friend of mine invited me to dinner. He fancied himself to be quite a chef and wanted to impress me. Well, he served me lamb with blueberry sauce and goat cheese. He sat across the table, watching me. "Well, what do you think?" he asked anxiously. I looked at him, groping for something to say, and the only thing I finally said, was, "Do I have to eat it?" It's good to be creative, but what if you create pleases only 1 percent of the people, you've failed. If it's too off the wall, no one's going to come back to eat at your restaurant. Now, whenever someone says, "Russell, I want you to try something I've made," I ask them to wrap it and I'll take it home.

First Flavor

'Ahi Katsu

wasabi-ginger butter sauce

Serves 4

8	oz.	'Ahi Block (sashimi grade)
4	sheets	Nori
1	bunch	Spinach (cleaned, stemmed, patted dry)
2	cups	Panko
2	each	Eggs
2	Tbsp	Water
1	cup	Flour
1	qt.	Vegetable Oil
		Salt & Pepper to taste

Wasabi-Ginger Butter Sauce -

1	each	Green Onion (chopped)
1	inch	Ginger (peeled and chopped)
1	Tbsp	Wasabi
1/4	cup	Rice Wine Vinegar
2	Tbsp	Soy Sauce
2	Tbsp	Heavy Cream
1/2	cup	Unsalted Butter (cut into cubes)

Method -

Cut 'Ahi into pieces the length of a *nori* wrapper and 1 inch thick. Spread *nori* sheets out. Line with spinach. Place one piece of 'Ahi on each sheet. Season with salt and pepper. Top again with spinach. Roll and seal the edge of the *nori* with water. Whip eggs with water and flour. Consistency should be that of a thin pancake batter. Put flour in one plate and *panko* in another. Roll wrapped 'Ahi into flour, then into batter mixture and then into the *panko* breading making sure all parts are covered.

Deep fry in hot oil (pre-heat to 350 degrees F.) until golden brown. Remove and slice. Ladle 1 oz. of sauce onto plate and arrange the 'Ahi slices on the plate.

Wasabi-Ginger Butter Sauce -

Place *green onion, ginger, wasabi* and rice wine vinegar in a sauce pan on medium heat and allow mixture to reduce by half. Add cream and reduce by half. Add *soy sauce* and turn to low heat. Whisk in butter cubes one at a time until incorporated. Remove from heat.

*I wanted to do 'Ahi in a more exotic way.
I put nori with it, spinach for color and
texture, then deep-fried it and created a
shoyu-wasabi sauce that went well with it.
It all just came out perfectly...*

'Ahi Poke Springroll with Wasabi Oil

Serves 6

1 lb	'Ahi, Grade 1 or 2, (cut into 1/4 inch pieces)
1/2 cup	*Green Onions* (chopped fine)
1/2 cup	Red Onions (chopped fine)
Pinch	Red Chilis (crushed)
1/2 cup	*Soy Sauce*
1-1/2 Tbsp	Sesame Seed Oil
1-1/2 in.	Fresh *Ginger* (grated)
1/4 cup	Sesame Seed (toasted)
12 sheets	*Menlo* Wrapper (spring roll wrapper)
1 each	Egg (beaten)
1 quart	Salad Oil (for frying)
	Salt & Pepper to taste

Wasabi Oil -

1/2 cup	Olive Oil
2 tsp	*Wasabi*

Method -

Mix all ingredients together except for the egg, *menlo* wrapper and frying oil. Season with salt and pepper. Let stand for about half an hour to release flavors.

Spoon about 1 heaping tablespoon of the 'Ahi mixture (*poke*) on to *menlo wrapper* and roll into a spring roll. Moisten the corner with the egg to seal the wrapper.

In pre-heated oil, fry for about 3 minutes at 350 degrees F. *Poke* should be medium rare on the inside.

Wasabi Oil -

In a small bowl, add olive oil and *Wasabi* together. Mix until smooth.

Calamari Salad
with garden vegetable dressing

Serves 4

Garden Vegetable Dressing -

1/2 medium	Carrot (*brunoisé*) finely diced 1 1/8" to 1/8" cubes	
1/2 medium	Red Bell Pepper (cleaned, seeded; *brunoisé*)	
1/2 medium	Green Bell Pepper (cleaned, seeded; *brunoisé*)	
1/2 medium	Red Onion (*brunoisé*)	
1 Tbsp	Minced Garlic	
1 whole	Dill Pickle (*brunoisé*)	
1/4 cup	Anchovie Filet (finely chopped)	
1/2 bunch	Parsley (chopped)	
2 Tbsp	Capers (chopped)	
8 cups	Mayonnaise	
1/2 cup	Red Wine Vinegar	
1-1/4 Tbsp	Worchestershire Sauce	
8 cups	Buttermilk	
	Salt & Pepper to taste	

Calamari -

1 lb	Calamari Tubes (cut tentacles into 3/4 inch pieces)
1/2 cup	Milk
1/3 cup	Fine Cornmeal
1 cup	All Purpose Flour
1 quart	Vegetable Oil
1/2 tsp	Black Pepper
1/8 tsp	Cayenne Pepper
1/4 tsp	Green Chili Powder

Method -

Soak calamari in milk for about 10 minutes, then strain. Mix all of the dry ingredients. Add calamari to the dry ingredients and coat well. Heat vegetable oil to 350 degrees F. Fry calamari for about 1 to 1-1/2 minutes, or until light brown or crispy if desired. Set on the side.

Garden Vegetable Dressing -

Combine all ingredients in a *non-reactive* bowl and mix until smooth. Season with salt and pepper.

To serve -

Toss salad with dressing. Place fried calamari on a plate in a circle and top with the tossed salad.

*This is a very decadent dish, which I prepared
in a really different way. The crunchiness of the
capers and onions, along with the caviar and 'Ahi,
gives it an awesome flavor . . . oh, to die for . . .*

'Ahi Tartar

tobiko caviar and wasabi oil

Serves 4

8	oz.	'Ahi, Grade I (very small diced)
4	Tbsp	Extra Virgin Olive Oil
1	Tbsp	*Green Onions* (chopped fine)
1	tsp	Capers (chopped)
1/2	tsp	*Ginger* (grated)
4	tsp	*Tobiko* Caviar
8	each	Tube Chives (for garnish)
1/4	cup	Olive Oil
1	tsp	*Wasabi*
		Salt & Pepper to taste

Method -

In a bowl, mix together all the ingredients except for the *wasabi* and extra virgin olive oil. Season with salt and pepper. A little more extra virgin olive oil may be needed if the mixture is too dry. In a small bowl, add olive oil and *wasabi* together. Mix until smooth.

In a martini glass, spoon about 2 oz. into the center. Drizzle *wasabi* oil over and garnish with *tobiko* caviar and tube chives.

'Ahi Carpaccio
wasabi aioli sauce

Serves 6

6	each	'Ahi, Grade 1 or 2 (1-1/2 oz. each)
1	Tbsp	Extra Virgin Olive Oil
2	each	*Green Onion* (chopped)
1	tsp	Black Sesame Seeds
1	tsp	*Nori*, Dried Seaweed (cut very fine – julienne)
1	each	Egg Yolk
1	cup	Salad Oil
1/2	clove	Garlic (minced)
1	tsp	*Wasabi*
		Salt & Pepper to taste

Method -

Place one piece of 'Ahi between sheets of plastic food wrap. Pound with a food hammer or a frying pan until 'Ahi is thin (about 1/4-inch thick). Remove one side of wrap and place the 'Ahi side down on plate. Remove wrapper and rub with extra virgin olive oil. Repeat with remaining 'Ahi pieces.

Prepare *aioli* in a food processor. Add egg, garlic and *wasabi*. Slowly drizzle in salad oil until mixture thickens. Remove from the food processor and season with salt and pepper.

Drizzle *aioli* over 'Ahi. Sprinkle with sesame seeds, *green onion* and *nori*.

*Remove wrapper and rub with extra virgin olive oil.

I was after something healthier with a different taste, but was still familiar to the local palate. It's pretty much the same as beef carpaccio and, like with the beef, we use only top grade 'Ahi . . .

Bruschetta, Mesclun of Greens

green onion vinaigrette

Serves 4

8	slices	French Bread (1-inch thick)
2	each	Ripe Large Tomatoes (seeded and diced)
4 - 6	leaves	Fresh Basil (chopped)
1	each	Large Clove Garlic (minced)
3	Tbsp	Extra Virgin Olive Oil
1/2	cup	Mesclun of Greens
1/4	cup	Champagne Vinegar
3/4	cup	Green Onions (diced)
1	small	Clove Garlic (minced)
1/4	tsp	Mustard (dry or poupon)
1/2	tsp	Honey
1/4	tsp	Ginger (chopped)
		Salt & Pepper to taste

Method -

In a large bowl combine tomatoes, basil, minced garlic and extra virgin olive oil. Season with salt and pepper. Let stand for about 2 to 3 hours in refrigerator before using.

Bake french bread in pre-heated oven at 300 degrees F. for about 6 minutes. Turn over and let bake for another 6 minutes. The bread can be grilled if at a barbeque. Top french bread with tomato mixture.

Vinaigrette -

Blend vinegar, *green onions*, garlic, mustard, honey and *ginger*. Season with salt and pepper.

Assembly -

Toss *mesclun* of greens with the vinaigrette. Place on plate. Garnish with the bruschetta.

Roasted Pepper Salad
balsamic vinaigrette

Serves 6

1	each	Red Bell Pepper
1	each	Green Bell Pepper
1	each	Yellow Bell Pepper
1	Head	Butter Lettuce
1	Tbsp	Capers

Balsamic Vinaigrette -

1/8 cup	Balsamic Vinegar
3/4 cup	Extra Virgin Olive Oil
1/2 clove	Garlic (minced)
1/2 tsp	Fresh Basil (finely chopped)
	Salt & Pepper to taste

Method -

Rub the red, green and yellow bell pepper with 1/4 cup olive oil and place on a sheet pan. Bake in pre-heated oven for about half an hour at 375 degrees F. Remove and place in stainless steel bowl and cover with clear food wrap. Let stand for about 15 minutes. Peel skin and remove seeds from peppers. Cut peppers into julienne strips (2 inches long, and 1/4 inch wide) and place in a non-reactive bowl.

Balsamic Vinaigrette -

In a *non-reactive* mixing bowl, combine the balsamic vinegar, 1/2 cup olive oil, garlic and basil. Season with salt and black pepper. Pour half of the vinaigrette mixture over the peppers and refrigerate for about 4 hours to marinate.

Line salad plate with butter lettuce and place a portion of the peppers in the middle. Drizzle with the remaining vinaigrette and garnish with the capers. Serve with toasted French bread.

35

Springroll of Duck Confit
plum chili sauce

Serves 6

1	pkg.	Springroll Wrapper
1/2	cup	Duck *Confit*
1	cup	Zucchini (julienne)
1	each	Red Bell Pepper (julienne)
1	each	Green Bell Pepper (julienne)
1	each	Round Onion (julienne)
1	tsp	*Fish Sauce*
1	Tbsp	*Oyster Sauce*
1	Tbsp	*Soy Sauce*
1	Clove	Garlic (chopped)
1/2	tsp	*Ginger* (chopped)
3	Tbsp	Cornstarch
3	Tbsp	Water
1	each	Egg
		Salt & Pepper to taste

Plum Chili Sauce -

1	cup	*Plum Sauce*
1/4	cup	Rice Wine Vinegar
1/8	cup	Sugar
1	Tbsp	Sweet Chili Sauce
2	tsp	*Fish Sauce*
2	Tbsp	*Chinese Parsley* (chopped)

Method -

In a medium-sized sauce pan, sauté duck confit, vegetables, garlic, and *ginger*. Add *fish sauce, oyster sauce* and *soy sauce*. Simmer and season with salt and pepper. Thicken slightly with cornstarch and water mixture. Let cool.

Roll in wrapper and moisten edges with the egg to seal. Deep fry until light brown, (about 3 minutes at 350 degrees F.)

Plum Chili Sauce -

Simmer rice wine vinegar and sugar until mixture is clear and slightly thick. Add *plum sauce*, chili sauce and *fish sauce*. Simmer for 3 minutes. Let cool then add chopped parsley.

I try not to be too wild in my flavoring. People have to already like that kind of food or get adjusted to it. I aim to please the general public, not just a small segment. I'm not trying to capture a niche market. I work a wider range of people.

The sweetness of the Chinese-style roast duck, combined with the liliko'i vinaigrette really goes well with the mesclun greens topped with crispy mooshoo wrappers . . . sort of an Asian tostada . . .

Chinese Barbeque Duck Salad
liliko'i vinaigrette

Serves 4

1	each	Duck, 4 1/2 - 5 lbs.
1	quart	Hot Water
1/8	cup	White Vinegar
1/4	bunch	Chinese Parsley
1/4	bunch	Green Onions
3	slices	Ginger Root
2	Tbsp	Soy Sauce
1/4	tsp	Five Spice Seasoning
1/2	cup	Water

Glaze -

2	cups	Plum Sauce
1	cup	Soy Sauce
1	cup	Hoisin Sauce
1	cup	Honey
1/4	Tbsp	Ginger (grated)
1/4	bunch	Chinese Parlsey
1/2	cup	Green Onions (chopped fine)

Liliko'i Vinaigrette -

1/2	each	Lime (zest and juice)
1	Tbsp	Sugar
1/2	tsp	Black Pepper (ground)
1	clove	Garlic (whole)
1/2	tsp	Ginger (chopped)
1	cup	Rice Wine Vinegar
3/4	cup	Liliko'i Purée (passion fruit)
3	cups	Salad Oil
1/4	cup	Honey

Method -

Put one quart hot water and vinegar mixture in a large pot and bring to a boil. Baste duck with boiling water for about 2 to 3 minutes, until skin of the duck feels tight.

In a stainless steel bowl, mash together the ginger, green onion and Chinese parsley. Add soy sauce, 1/2 cup water and five spice seasoning. Rub the duck inside and out very well. Hang duck in a cool area until skin is dry (about 7 to 8 hours).

Roast duck in a pre-heated oven at 325 degrees F. for about 1 hour. (Duck should be a light brown.) Remove from oven and cool.

Glaze -

In a stainless steel bowl, add Chinese parsley and green onion. Mash with the back of a spoon. Add the rest of the ingredients and mix well.

Liliko'i Vinaigrette -

Add the ingredients in a blender and blend until smooth. Add oil slowly, then the honey. Do not over mix.

Final Procedure -

Remove duck breast from the duck. Brush with glaze and return to oven and bake at previous 350 degree F. temperature. When duck is a rich, golden brown, remove and slice.

In a mixing bowl, add mesclun of greens and some Liliko'i vinaigrette (approximately 1 oz. per person). Toss and garnish with sliced duck.

Clam and Corn Chowder

Serves 12

4	strips	Bacon (diced)
1/4	cup	Green Bell Peppers (diced small)
1/2	cup	Onions (diced small)
1/4	cup	Celery (diced small)
1/2	tsp	Thyme (fresh and chopped or 1/4 tsp dried)
1/2	cup	Butter
1/2	cup	All Purpose Flour
3	cups	Clam Juice or Stock
2	cups	Chopped Clams
1	cup	Corn Kernels
1-1/2	cup	Potatoes (peeled, diced and cooked separately)
1	cup	Cream
		Worcestershire Sauce to taste
		Tabasco to taste
		Salt & Pepper to taste

Method -

Render bacon in a large sauce pan. Add onion, celery, peppers and sauté until translucent. Add thyme and butter.

When butter is melted, add flour and stir constantly over low heat. Do not brown mixture.

Slowly add clam juice while continuously stirring with a wire whip. Bring to a boil. Simmer for about 15 minutes or until flour is cooked though.

Add chopped clams, corn and cooked potatoes. Bring to a simmer. Add cream and bring to a simmer. Season with worcestershire-shire, tabasco, salt and pepper.

Portuguese Bean Soup

Serves 20

3/4 cup	Dried Kidney Beans (soaked over night in water)
2	each	*Portuguese Sausage* (6 oz.)
1	each	Ham Hock (smoked)
1	can	Tomatoes, or 2 cups Fresh Tomatoes
1/2 cup	Carrots (diced large)
1	cup	Onions (diced large)
3/4 cup	Celery (diced large)
1/2 cup	Bell Pepper (diced large)
2	cups	Cabbage (diced large)
1	Tbsp	Garlic (chopped)
1	tsp	*Ginger* (chopped)
1	each	Bay Leaf
1	tsp	Paprika
1/8 tsp	Marjoram
1/8 tsp	Basil
2	qts.	Beef or Chicken Stock
1	cup	Potato (diced)
		Salt & Pepper to taste

Method -

Rinse and soak beans overnight. In a large pot on low heat, add 1 tablespoon oil. Sauté the sausage until fat is rendered. Increase heat and add the diced vegetables (except cabbage and tomato) and sauté until transparent (approximately 5 minutes). Add garlic, *ginger* and herbs.

Stir and sauté for about 2 minutes. Add stock and ham hock and simmer for about 1 hour. Add beans about half an hour after stock boils. When beans are soft, add cabbage and tomatoes and continue to cook. Remove the ham hock and dice. Add back to soup and season with salt and pepper.

Chinese Chicken Salad
hoisin dressing

Serves 4

1/2 lb	Mesclun Mix	
1 pkg.	Soba Noodles	
1/2 each	Red Onion (sliced thin)	
1 each	Carrot (shredded)	
1/2 bunch	Green Onions (julienne)	
2 each	Chicken Breast (boneless)	
8 each	Won Ton Pi, Fried Pasta Sheets (julienne)	
1 Tbsp	Black Sesame Seeds	
1 cup	Rice Vinegar	

Hoisin Dressing -

1/2 cup	Hoisin Sauce
1/2 cup	Lemon Juice
3/4 cup	Salad Oil
1/4 cup	Sesame Oil
1/4 cup	Rice Vinegar
3 Tbsp	Sugar

Method -

Soak sliced red onions in rice vinegar for half an hour.

Grill chicken breasts and set aside until needed.

Toss *mesclun* mix with about 1/2 cup Hoisin Dressing. Portion out onto 6 plates.

Toss *soba* noodles with dressing and portion out into 6 equal parts. Place *soba* noodles on lettuce.

Hoisin Dressing -

Mix all ingredients together until emulsified.

To serve -

Place marinated onions on *soba* noodles. Top with shredded carrots and julienne *green onion*. Slice chicken breast and divide into six portions. Arrange chicken around salad. Sprinkle *won ton pi* around the perimeter of the plate. Garnish with black sesame seeds.

We developed this dish by starting with a Chinese chicken
salad and a Japanese somen salad. We crossed that line
by substituting somen noodles with soba, because
we felt the soba noodles had more texture. . .
Again, we didn't want to be like everyone else . . .

Rock Shrimp, Sliced Tomatoes and Macadamia Nut Pesto Quesadilla

Serves 4

1/2 cup	Fresh Basil (chopped)
1/2 cup	Parmesan Cheese (finely grated)
2 cloves	Garlic (minced)
1/8-1/4 cup	*Macadamia Nuts*
1/2 cup	Olive Oil
4 each	*Mooshoo* Wrapper or Flour Tortillas
24 slices	Roma Tomatoes (sliced)
1-1/2 cup	Rock Shrimp
2 cup	Provolone Cheese (grated)
1/4 cup	Garlic Butter
	Fresh Basil (to garnish)
	Salt & Pepper to taste

Pesto -

In a blender, add the basil, garlic, *macadamia nuts* and olive oil. Blend until smooth. Add cheese in slowly until mixture thickens. Season with salt and pepper.

Method -

Top each *mooshoo* wrapper with tomato slices and shrimp. Drizzle pesto over the *mooshoo*. Top with cheese. Repeat with the other four.

Heat skillet and add garlic butter. Place the finished *mooshoo* into the pan. Remove pan from heat and place in pre-heated oven at 350 degrees F. for about 8 minutes, or until shrimp is cooked and the sides of the *mooshoo* are lightly browned. Cut and garnish with basil.

Mesclun of Greens with Ricotta Salata
balsamic vinaigrette

Serves 6

3/4 cup	Mesclun of Greens
1/4 cup	Balsamic Vinegar
3/4 cup	Extra Virgin Olive Oil
1/4 tsp	Garlic (chopped)
1/2 tsp	Basil (finely chopped)
1-1/2 cup	Ricotta Salata
	Salt & Pepper to taste

Method -

In a stainless steel bowl, combine vinegar, oil, garlic and basil. Whisk until mixture emulsifies. Season with salt and pepper.

In another bowl, add the *mesclun* of greens mix. Add vinaigrette and toss. Garnish with *Ricotta Salata*. Roma tomatoes and Greek olives could be added to give the salad more *zest*.

Pan Seared Sashimi Salad

Serves 4

1	cup	*Mesclun* of Greens
1/2	cup	*Daikon* (julienne)
1/2	cup	Cucumber (julienne)
1/2	cup	Carrot (julienne)
1/2	cup	Zucchini (julienne)
1/2	cup	Potato Sticks
8	slices	*Ginger* Chips

Dressing -

3/4	cup	*Soy Sauce*
3	cups	Salad Oil
1	cup	Rice Vinegar
4	each	Lemons (juice)
1/8	cup	*Ponzu Sauce*
3/4	cup	Sesame Oil
1	cup	Sugar
1/4	cup	Sesame Seeds (toasted)

Sashimi -

8	oz.	'Ahi (Sashimi) Grade I
1	tsp	Coriander (cracked)
1	tsp	Black Pepper (cracked)
2	Tbsp	*Chinese Parsley* (chopped)
2	Tbsp	*Green Onions* (chopped)
3	Tbsp	Peanut Oil

Method -

Mix together coriander, pepper, *Chinese parsley* and *green onions*. Roll 'Ahi into mixture coating all sides. Heat pan until hot and add peanut oil. Place 'Ahi in pan and sear until golden brown on all sides. Do not overcook. 'Ahi should be rare on the inside. Chill; set aside until needed.

Dressing -

In a mixing bowl, combine salad oil, rice vinegar, lemon juice, *ponzu sauce*, sesame oil, *soy sauce*, sugar, and toasted sesame seeds to create dressing.

In another bowl, toss together the *mesclun* of greens, julienne of vegetables, and some of the dressing. Garnish with slices of 'Ahi around the greens and top with *ginger* chips.

Warm Spinach Salad
pancetta-tarragon vinaigrette

Serves 6

I	bunch	Spinach (washed and destemmed)
I	cup	Mushrooms (sliced)
I	cup	Tomatoes (diced)
I/2	cup	Hard Cooked Egg (chopped)
I	cup	Artichoke Hearts (I/4 cut)
I	cup	Warm *Pancetta-Tarragon* Vinaigrette

Pancetta-Tarragon Vinaigrette -

I/4	cup	*Pancetta*, or Bacon (diced)
I/4	cup	Onion (diced fine)
I	Tbsp	Garlic (chopped)
I	Tbsp	Mustard (dijon)
I/2	tsp	Basil (chopped or pinch of dried)
I/4	tsp	Tarragon (chopped or pinch of dried)
3/4	cup	Olive Oil
I	Tbsp	Honey
I/4	cup	Red Wine Vinegar
		Salt & Pepper to taste

Method -

Place spinach in a large bowl and set aside.

In a large sauté pan, heat the vinaigrette. Add artichoke hearts, mushrooms and tomatoes and stir gently. Pour the warm mixture over the spinach. With tongs, toss the spinach with the vinaigrette. Place on plate and garnish with chopped egg.

Pancetta-Tarragon Vinaigrette -

In a small sauce pan, render bacon over medium heat until half way cooked. Add onion and garlic and continue to sauté until translucent. Deglaze with red wine vinegar and add herbs and mustard. Let steep a few minutes. Add oil and season with honey and salt and pepper.

Indonesian Sambol Dressing

Serves 6

1	Tbsp	*Ginger*
1	Tbsp	Chili (fresh)
1	tsp	Garlic
1	tsp	*Shrimp Paste*
2	Tbsp	Coriander Seeds
1/4 cup		Lime (juice)
1/4 cup		Sugar
1/4 cup		Molasses
1/2 cup		Peanut Oil
		Salt & Pepper to taste

Method -

Add all ingredients in a blender and blend until smooth. Best served with these vegetables: julienne cabbage, carrots, chopped peanuts and bean sprouts.

Pan Fried Scallops with Mesclun Greens
liliko'i vinaigrette

Serves 4

Liliko'i Vinaigrette -

1/2 each	Lime (*zest* and meat only)	
1 Tbsp	Sugar	
1/2 tsp	Black Pepper (ground)	
1 clove	Garlic (whole)	
1/2 tsp	*Ginger* (chopped)	
1 cup	Rice Wine Vinegar	
3/4 cup	*Liliko'i* (passion fruit) Purée	
3 cups	Salad Oil	
1/4 cup	Honey	

Scallops -

1/2 cup	*Mesclun* of Greens	
12 each	Sea Scallops 20 - 30 count	
1/2 cup	Butter (clarified)	
1/4 cup	Flour	
	Salt & Pepper to taste	

Liliko'i Vinaigrette -

Combine all ingredients in a blender and blend until smooth. Chill.

Method -

Heat pan, then add butter. Season scallops with salt and pepper. Dredge in flour and shake off excess. Pan fry scallops until golden brown and turn over. Sear until a golden brown. Remove to a plate lined with a paper towel to remove excess oil.

Toss greens with vinaigrette and arrange scallops around lettuce.

Drizzle with vinaigrette.

Shrimp and Taro Cake
banana salsa

Serves 6

Taro Cake -

1	cup	Rock Shrimp (peeled, deveined and chopped)
3	cups	Cooked *Taro* (grated coarse)
1/4	cup	*Green Onions* (chopped)
1/4	tsp	Garlic (minced)
1/4	tsp	*Ginger* (grated)
1/8	cup	Onions (minced)
1	Tbsp	Fresh Basil (chopped)
1	Tbsp	Cognac
2	Tbsp	Cornstarch
1/8	tsp	Cayenne Pepper
2	each	Egg Whites (well beaten)
		Salt & Pepper to taste

Banana Salsa -

1	cup	Ripe Banana (diced)
1/8	cup	Red Bell Pepper (diced, ribbed and seeded)
1/4	cup	Onion (finely diced)
1	each	Jalapeno (seeded and minced)
1/8	tsp	*Cumin* Seed (ground)
1/2	tsp	Fresh Oregano (chopped)
1	Tbsp	*Chinese Parsley* (chopped)
1	tsp	Fresh Basil (chopped)
1	each	Lime (juice)

Method -

In a mixing bowl, combine all ingredients except *taro*. Fold in the eggs whites. Add the *taro*, season with salt and pepper and mix. Set mixture aside for 10 minutes. Form into patties. In a medium sauté pan, sauté until golden brown on both sides. Garnish with salsa and *taro* chips.

Banana Salsa -

In a mixing bowl, combine all ingredients and refrigerate for 1 hour before serving. Note: Place plastic wrap directly over the salsa bowl before refrigerating to retard the browning of the bananas.

Waipio Valley is a beautiful, undeveloped valley known
for its taro farms, so I thought to myself: "Everyone does a
rock shrimp with potato. What if I used taro?"
I created a banana salsa to go with the dish and it
dove-tailed together beautifully . . .

Filets of Prosciutto Wrapped Beef
grilled portabello mushrooms

Serves 4

4	each	Beef Tenderloin (8 oz. each)
8	each	*Prosciutto* Ham (thinly sliced)
4	each	*Portabello* Mushrooms
1/8 cup		Balsamic Vinegar
3/8 cup		Olive Oil
1/4 tsp		Garlic (minced)
		Salt & Pepper to taste

Portabello Mushrooms -

In a stainless steel bowl, mix together balsamic vinegar, olive oil and garlic. Season with salt and pepper. Cut mushrooms in half and marinate in mixture for about 3 hours.

Beef Tenderloin-

Wrap filets with 2 slices of prosciutto ham. Use toothpicks to secure ham in place. Season with salt and pepper.

Grill filet over charcoal until desired doneness. When meat is about done to your liking, grill mushrooms for about 3 minutes per side.

Place filets on top of mushrooms and serve.

You can't really ruin a filet of beef,
but you can add to it and enhance it.
People perceive bacon as being too fatty, so
we wrapped the filet with prosciutto. The
filet has a pleasantly chewier texture,
the flavors go together really well. . .

Asian Style Osso Bucco

Serves 4

Method -

4	each	Osso Bucco, Veal Shank (cut 2 inches)
1/4	cup	All Purpose Flour
2	Tbsp	Peanut Oil
1/4	cup	White Wine
3	cups	Veal Stock
1-1/2	inch	*Ginger* Root (peeled and sliced)
1	each	*Star Anise*
1/2	cup	Tomatoes (diced)
1/2	cup	Fresh *Shiitake* Mushrooms (sliced)
1	Tbsp	*Soy Sauce*
1	tsp	Orange (*zest*)
1	Tbsp	Lemon (juice)
1/4	cup	Water
2	Tbsp	Cornstarch
		Salt & Pepper to taste

Preheat roasting pan. Lightly flour the veal shank on both sides. Add the peanut oil to the pan and sauté the veal shank until golden brown on both sides. Add the rest of the ingredients except for the cornstarch and water. Bring to a boil and cover. Place in pre-heated oven at 350 degrees F. and let it braise for about 2 hours. Remember to check the veal after about 1-1/2 hours, since some ovens run a little hot. The meat should be soft to the touch and slightly away from the bone. When the veal is done, remove the meat from the pan, set aside and keep warm.

Mix together cornstarch and water to a smooth paste and add slowly to the boiling stock. Let simmer for about 4 minutes. Season with salt and black pepper. Strain and ladle sauce over veal shank before serving.

Angel Hair Pasta with Macadamia Nut Pesto

Serves 4

1/2 cup	Basil (Chopped)
1/2 cup	Parmesan Cheese (grated fine)
2 each	Clove Garlic
1/2 cup	Olive Oil
1/8 -1/4 cup	*Macadamia* Nuts (coarse chop)
12 oz.	Capellini - Dry (Angel Hair Pasta)
	Salt & Pepper to taste

Method -

In a blender, add all ingredients except the pasta and the cheese. Blend until smooth. Add cheese in slowly until mixture thickens. Consistency of pesto should be that of pancake batter. Season with salt and pepper. Cook pasta in boiling water. Strain and mix with pesto. Top with cheese and serve.

Penne with Portuguese Sausage, Tomatoes & Red Onion

Serves 4

8	oz.	*Portuguese Sausage*, 1/4-inch thick (sliced)
2	each	Roma Tomatoes (chopped)
1	each	Red Onion (chopped)
12	oz.	Penne (dry)
2	Tbsp	Olive Oil
1	Tbsp	Basil (chopped)
2	cloves	Garlic (chopped)
4	Tbsp	Parmesan Cheese (grated)
1/8	cup	White Wine
1	Tbsp	Balsamic Vinegar
		Salt & Pepper to taste

Method -

Sauté *portuguese sausage* in a sauté pan until sausage is almost fully cooked. Drain oil from pan. Add olive oil, onions and tomatoes. Simmer for about 2 minutes. Add garlic, basil, white wine and balsamic vinegar. Let cook for about 3 minutes. Toss in cooked penne pasta and simmer until heated through. Season with salt and pepper. Add half the amount of cheese and toss. Portion into 4 plates and top with remainder of the cheese.

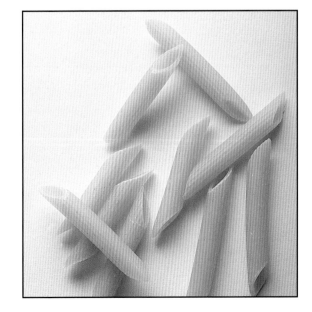

Assorted Seafood with Pan Fried Angel Hair Pasta
tobiko caviar cream sauce

Serves 4

1/4 cup	Crab Meat
8 each	Scallop or Mussels
8 each	Shrimp
4 oz.	Fish
3-4 oz.	Capellini - Dry (Angel hair Pasta)
2 Tbsp	Olive Oil
2 cups	Whipping Cream or Avocet
1 tsp	*Ginger*
1/2 tsp	*Soy Sauce*
1/4 tsp	Garlic
1 Tbsp	*Tobiko* Caviar
2 Tbsp	*Green Onions*
1 tsp	Black Sesame Seeds
	Salt & Pepper to taste

Method -

At medium heat, pour whipping cream in a sauce pot and reduce to half its volume, or until cream thickens. When cream is at the right consistency, add *ginger*, garlic and *soy sauce*. These ingredients can be increased or lessened.

In a large pot, boil water and angel hair pasta. Be careful not to overcook. Keep it slightly under done (al denté). When pasta is done, rinse under cold water and drain thoroughly. Add olive oil and toss until pasta is coated. Heat frying pan then add a little olive oil. Take a handful of pasta and place in a pan pressing it flat at the same time. Pan fry until brown on one side and turn. Do not stack pasta when done.

Heat sauté pan. Add oil. Sauté shrimp, scallops and fish. When the seafood is about 3/4 cooked, add the cream mixture, *green onions* and *tobiko* caviar (reserve some for garnish). As soon as mixture boils, let it simmer for about 1 minute. Add crab meat and season.

To Serve -

Place fried pasta on a plate. Spoon equal portions of seafood on each plate. Top with the cream, *tobiko* caviar and sprinkle with black sesame seeds for garnish.

Linguine with Island Chicken

Serves 4

2	cups	Heavy Cream
1-1/2	Tbsp	*Soy Sauce*
3/4	Tbsp	Chili Sauce
1/4	Tbsp	H*oisin* Sauce
1/4	cup	*Shiso* Leaf (julienned)
2	each	Chicken Breast (boneless and skinless)
1	each	Japanese Eggplant (halved lengthwise, grilled and sliced diagonally 1/2-inch thick)
8	each	*Shiitake* Mushrooms (stemmed and sliced)
1/2	cup	Oven Roasted or Sun Dried Tomatoes (chopped)
1	Tbsp	Garlic (minced)
1/4	tsp	Pepper (crushed)
1	Tbsp	Peanut Oil
3/4	lb	Linguine (dried)
		Salt & Pepper to taste

Method -

Heat a frying pan and add peanut oil. Brown chicken pieces in hot peanut oil over medium high heat. Add eggplant, *shiitake* mushrooms, tomatoes, garlic, crushed red pepper and sauté for about 2 minutes. Add heavy cream and reduce by 1/4. Add *soy sauce*, chili sauce, *hoisin* sauce and *shiso* leaf. Add salt and black pepper. Add cooked linguine and simmer for about 1 minute. Serve immediately.

Sake Glazed Shrimp with Hong Kong Noodles

Serves 4

28	pcs.	Shrimp 21-25 count (peeled and deveined)
1/2	cup	Green Bell Pepper (cut into 1/2 inch squares; seeded and ribbed)
1/2	cup	Red Bell Pepper (cut into 1/2 inch squares; seeded and ribbed)
1/2	cup	Red Onion (chopped)
1	cup	*Green Onion* (cut on bias to garnish)
1	tsp	Garlic (chopped)
1/2	cup	Sake
1	cup	*Teriyaki* Sauce (slightly thickened with corn starch)
1	tsp	Sesame Seeds (toasted)
4	bunches	Hong Kong Noodles

Teriyaki Sauce -

1/4	cup	Sugar
1/4	cup	Sake
1/2	cup	*Soy Sauce*
1	cup	*Mirin*
2	Tbsp	Cornstarch
2	Tbsp	Water

Method -

In a large sauté pan, heat 2 tablespoons oil. Add shrimp and sauté on one side. Season with salt and pepper. Turn over shrimp and season. Add garlic and toss. Add bell peppers and red onions and stir. Fry until shrimp is done.

Deglaze with sake and add *teriyaki* sauce. Cook slightly.

Teriyaki Sauce -

In a medium sauce pot, combine all ingredients and heat until dissolved. Thicken with cornstarch and water mixture.

Noodles -

In a large sauce pan, heat 2 inches (depth) of oil. Loosen the noodle bundles and fry in oil until crisp. Turn over and fry again until crisp. Drain on paper towel.

To serve-

Place shrimp on crisp noodles and pour sauce over. Garnish with *green onion* and toasted sesame seeds.

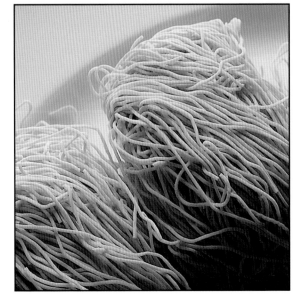

Black Mushroom Ravioli
basil cream sauce

Serves 8

2	cups	Fresh *Shiitake* Mushrooms (stems removed)
2	cups	Button Mushrooms
I	tsp	Garlic (chopped)
2	Tbsp	*Green Onion* (chopped)
3	Tbsp	Butter
32	pcs.	*Won Ton Pi*
1/2	cup	*Panko* or Fresh Bread Crumbs
		Salt & Pepper to taste

Basil Sauce -

1/2	cup	White Wine
2	Tbsp	Basil (julienne)
2-1/2	cup	Heavy Cream
1/2	tsp	Garlic (chopped)
I	tsp	*Green Onions* (chopped)
2	Tbsp	Butter (unsalted)

Method -

Grate mushrooms on a medium grater (this can be done by hand or with a food processor). In a large sauté pan on medium heat, melt the butter. Add the garlic and *green onions* and sauté until translucent. Add the mushrooms and sauté until the water starts to come out. Turn heat down to medium and continue to cook stirring occasionally. Once the liquid has evaporated, season to taste with salt and pepper. Add enough *panko* to bind (approximately 1/2 cup). Spread out on a cookie sheet to cool.

Ravioli -

Lay out *won ton pi* and brush with water. Place I tablespoon of mushroom filling in the middle. Lightly moisten another *won ton pi* and place over mixture lining up the *won ton pi* so it is square. Press to adhere.

To Cook Ravioli -

Place ravioli in boiling, lightly salted, water for 2 minutes. Drain and serve.

In a sauce pot over medium high, heat I tablespoon of basil, white wine, *green onions* and garlic. Reduce by half and add the heavy cream. Reduce until thick and add butter. Season with salt and pepper. Strain through a sieve and add I tablespoon of basil.

Actually, when you think about it, it's possible that the Italians got the idea for ravioli from the Chinese won ton when Marco Polo returned from China.

Cornmeal Crusted Calamari
creole mustard sauce

Serves 4

4	each	Calamari Steaks (5 - 6 oz. each, pounded out)
1	cup	Milk
1	cup	Cornmeal
1/4	cup	Butter (clarified)
		Salt & Pepper to taste

Creole Mustard Sauce -

1	Tbsp	*Green Onions* (minced)
1/2	cup	White Wine
1	Tbsp	Worchestershire Sauce
2	Tbsp	Creole Mustard
1/4	cup	Heavy Cream
1	Tbsp	Capers
1/2	cup	Unsalted Butter (cubed)

Method -

Place calamari steak on a cutting board and pound with a meat tenderizer. Place in a bowl with milk. Mix salt, pepper and corn meal in a flat pan. Coat both sides of the calamari with cornmeal. Sauté in clarified butter over medium high heat.

Place on plate and pour sauce on each steak.

Creole Mustard Sauce -

Combine *green onions*, white wine and worchestershire sauce in a sauce pan. Reduce by one half. Add heavy cream, mustard and capers. Reduce heat to low. Whisk in butter, one cube at a time. Keep warm in a double boiler until ready to serve.

Ama Ebi & Scallop Ravioli
lobster ginger sauce

Serves 6

Ravioli -

18	each	Ama Ebi
12	pieces	Sea Scallops
8	pieces	Shiitake Mushrooms, (Brunoise)
1/4	cup	Green Onions (finely diced)
		Salt & Pepper to taste
18	pieces	Won Ton Pi - (pasta sheets)
1	cup	Peanut oil

Beurre Blanc -

1/2	each	Round Onion (sliced)
1	cup	White Wine
2	cups	Butter
		Salt & Pepper to taste

Lobster - Ginger Sauce -

1-1/4	qt.	Lobster Stock
2	Tbsp	Tomato Paste
1/2	inch	Fresh Ginger Root
1	inch	Crystallized Ginger Root

Method -

In a sauce pan, slowly heat the peanut oil. Add shrimp and scallops and cook until it turns white. Remove and drain. Dice shrimp and scallops into small chunks. Add *green onion, shiitake* mushrooms and about half of the beurre blanc. Mix and season with salt and pepper. Spoon about a tablespoon onto the center of the *won ton pi*. Lightly moisten another *won ton pi* with water and place over the mixture lining up the *won ton pi* so it is square. Press to adhere. Cut out the ravioli using a round cutter. Place on sheet pan dusted with cornstarch. Place in refrigerator until time of usage.

Beurre Blanc -

Cook onions with a tablespoon of clarified butter. Add white wine and reduce to half. Slowly whisk in butter. Season with salt and pepper. Strain and keep warm.

Lobster - Ginger Sauce -

In a sauce pan reduce lobster stock by 25% of volume. Add tomato paste and two types of *ginger*. Simmer for about 20 minutes. Strain and keep hot.

Assembly -

Place ravioli in boiling water. Let simmer for about 3 minutes. Remove and place in stainless steel bowl. Add beurre blanc and toss lightly. Place ravioli in pasta bowl and ladle lobster sauce over each ravioli. Serve immediately.

Nori Wrapped Mahimahi

over soba, ginger & soy vinaigrette

Serves 4

Mahimahi -

4	each	*Mahimahi* Filets (6 oz. each)
1	piece	Yaki Sushi *Nori* (dry seaweed, cut into 3/4 inch each)
		Cooking Oil

Teriyaki -

1	cup	*Mirin*
1/2	cup	*Soy Sauce*
1/4	cup	Sugar
1/4	cup	Sake

Soba Salad -

1	8 oz. pkg.	*Soba* Noodles (cooked)
1/4	cup	Carrots (julienne)
1/4	cup	Cucumber (julienne)
1/4	cup	Zucchini (julienne)

Ginger Soy Vinaigrette -

3	Tbsp	Sesame Oil
3	Tbsp	*Soy Sauce*
1	Tbsp	Sesame Seeds (toasted)
1	each	Lemon (juice)
2	Tbsp	Sugar
1-1/2	cup	Salad Oil
2	tsp	*Ponzu* Vinegar
1/2	tsp	*Ginger* (grated)

Mahimahi -

Wrap *mahimahi* with *nori* strips and set aside until needed.

Teriyaki -

Dissolve ingredients in sauce pan over low heat and set aside until needed.

Ginger Soy Vinaigrette -

Mix all ingredients in a bowl and set aside until needed.

Toss *soba* and vegetables with vinaigrette and divide onto plates.

Pan sear *mahimahi* in sauté pan with small amount of cooking oil until golden brown on both sides.

Just before *mahimahi* is completely cooked, add *teriyaki* to glaze fish. Place fish over noodles. Garnish with *green onions*.

We actually started by calling this a "mahi musubi,"
because here in Hawai'i, we have something called a
Spam musubi. We played around with the idea and
wrapped the mahimahi like a musubi.
We elevated it to a higher level . . .

Grilled Mahimahi
lime butter sauce and tropical relish

Serves 6

6   each   *Mahimahi* Filets
                (6 1/2 oz. each)

Tropical Relish -

1   each   Hayden Mango
                (peeled, seeded and
                diced)

1/2 cup   Pineapple (diced)

1/2 cup   Papaya (peeled,
                seeded and diced)

1   Tbsp   *Chinese parsley*
                (chopped)

1/2 tsp   Oregano
                (fresh and chopped)

1/4 tsp   *Cumin* (ground)

1/4 tsp   Garlic (chopped)

2   tsp   Lime (juice)

1/2 each   Jalapeno Pepper

               Salt & Pepper to taste

Lime Butter Sauce -

1/2 cup   White Wine

1/4 cup   Rice Wine Vinegar

1   Tbsp   *Green Onions*

1   tsp   Lime (*zest*)

1/4 cup   Heavy Cream

1   cup   Butter

2   each   Limes (juice)

               Salt & Pepper to taste

Tropical Relish -

In a bowl, add mango, pineapple, papaya, *chinese parsley*, oregano, *cumin*, garlic, lime juice and diced jalapeno. Season with salt and pepper.

Lime Butter Sauce -

In a sauce pan, add white wine, lime juice, *green onions*, lime *zest*, and rice wine vinegar. Reduce by half. Add heavy cream and reduce by half. Add softened butter a little at a time stirring constantly. Strain through a sieve and season with salt and pepper.

To serve -

Grill *mahimahi*. Ladle 1 oz. sauce on plate. Place *mahimahi* on top of sauce and top with tropical relish.

72

Baked Mahimahi
with oven dried tomatoes and roasted garlic broth

Serves 6

6	each	*Mahimahi* Filets (6 oz. each)
1	cup	Fresh Bread Crumbs or *Panko*
14	leaves	Spinach (cleaned & stemmed)
4	cups	Veal Stock
3	Tbsp	Salad Oil
1/4	cup	Bacon (finely diced)
1	each	Garlic
1	Tbsp	*Green Onions* (chopped)
1/4	cup	White Wine
1	sprig	Fresh Thyme
1	Tbsp	Olive Oil
2	Tbsp	Butter
		Salt & Pepper to taste

Oven Dried Tomatoes -

2	each	Tomatoes (cut into wedges)

Oven Dried Tomatoes -

Bake tomatoes in pre-heated oven at 250 degrees F. for 4 hours.

Broth -

In a sauce pan, sauté bacon until most of the fat is rendered. Drain excess fat. Add white wine, *green onions* and garlic. Reduce by half of the amount. Add veal stock, thyme and oven dried tomatoes. Simmer for about half an hour. Whisk in butter and add spinach right before service and season with salt and pepper.

Fish -

Rub *mahimahi* with olive oil and season with salt and pepper. Top with the fresh bread crumbs or *panko* (thin and even crust atop *mahimahi*). Place on lightly greased baking sheet. Repeat with the rest of the filets. Bake in pre-heated oven at 350 degrees F. for about 10 to 15 minutes, depending upon the doneness desired.

To serve -

Ladle sauce into a pasta dish and place *mahimahi* in the center. With tongs or a fork, place some of the spinach and dried tomato mixture around the *mahimahi*. Garnish with a sprig of thyme or parsley. (Mashed potatoes are a good accompaniment for this dish).

Chinese Steamed 'Opakapaka
with black bean sauce

Serves 4

4	each	'Opakapaka Filets (7 oz. each)
1	cup	All Purpose Flour
3	Tbsp	Chinese Black Beans (salted)
1/2	cup	Ginger (julienne)
2	bunches	Chinese parsley
1	quart	Chicken Stock
1-1/2	Tbsp	Oyster Sauce
3/4	Tbsp	Soy Sauce
3/4	Tbsp	Sesame Oil
4	Tbsp	Peanut Oil
1/4	cup	Cornstarch
1/4	cup	Green Bell Pepper (julienne)
1	cup	Onion
1/4	cup	Water
		Salt & Pepper to taste
1/4	cup	Green Onions (julienne)

Method -

In a medium sized pot, bring chicken stock, *soy sauce, oyster sauce* and sesame oil to a boil.

Mix together 1/4 cup cornstarch and 1/4 cup water and add to thicken the chicken stock mixture. Set aside until needed.

Lightly flour 'Opakapaka and season with salt and pepper.

Heat skillet, then add peanut oil. Add floured 'Opakapaka and pan sear until golden brown on one side. Turn fish and add chicken stock mixture to skillet and place in pre-set oven at 350 degrees F. for 8 to 10 minutes or to desired doneness of fish. Remove skillet from oven. Remove fish and place them on a large serving platter.

Place skillet back on stove at medium heat and add black beans and simmer for about 3 more minutes. Add the *ginger*, bell pepper and *green onions* and simmer for 1 minute. Adjust seasoning. Spoon over 'Opakapaka filets and top with vegetables and *chinese parsley*.

I first prepared this dish with a whole kalekale, but, unfortunately, most people don't like to deal with bones in their fish, or the head of a fish on their plate, so we used fileted 'Opakapaka, which worked well and was also easier to get all year 'round . . .

Jasmine Tea Steamed Filet of 'Opakapaka
coriander butter sauce

Serves 4

4	each	'Opakapaka Filets (6 1/2 oz. each)
1	cup	Bread Crumbs (fresh)
1	Tbsp	*Chinese parsley* (finely chopped, save stems until needed)
2	bags	Jasmine Tea - 3 cups water
1	Tbsp	Coriander Seeds
1	cup	Butter
1/8	cup	White Wine
1	Tbsp	*Ginger* (grated)
1	tsp	*Ginger* (chopped)
1/8	cup	Rice Wine Vinegar
1/4	cup	Heavy Cream
1	bunch	*Green Onions*
		Salt & Pepper to taste

Jasmine Tea -

Steep tea with water. Strain and set aside until needed. Grind bread crumbs in food processor until fine. Add grated *ginger* and chopped *Chinese parsley* to bread crumbs.

Sauce -

Heat coriander seeds, chopped ginger, white wine, rice wine vinegar and *Chinese parsley* stems and reduce by half. Add heavy cream and reduce to one half.

Add butter, a tablespoon at a time, stirring constantly over low heat. (If heat is too high, the sauce will break). Remove from stove and strain. Season with salt and pepper.

Method -

Season 'Opakapaka with salt and pepper and top with seasoned bread crumbs. Place in perforated pan (double boiler). Put tea in pot and place the perforated pan over it. Cover and steam for about 12 minutes. Time may vary depending upon the cut (thickness) of the fish.

When done, remove from pan. Place 4 tablespoons of sauce on plate and place fish in the center. Garnish with vegetables and julienne of *green onions*.

Pan Seared Filet of 'Opakapaka
shiso scented mashed potatoes, carrot infusion

Serves 6

6	each	'Opakapaka Filets (6 oz. each, skin on)
4	each	Potatoes (peeled and boiled)
1/2	cup	Heavy Cream
4	Tbsp	Butter
3	each	Shiso Leaf (diced fine)
1	cup	Carrot Juice
2	Tbsp	Rice Wine Vinegar
2	stalks	Green Onions for garnish
		Salt & Pepper to taste

Method -

Whip potatoes and add cream, butter and *shiso* leaf. Season with salt and pepper. Cover with foil and keep warm.

In a medium sauce pot, reduce carrot syrup (juice) and rice wine vinegar by half and set aside.

Season 'Opakapaka filets with salt and pepper. Pan sear (skin side down) for about 2 minutes, or until brown. Turn filet over and cook for another 2 to 3 minutes. Remove and place over 1 scoop of mashed potatoes. Drizzle the carrot syrup around the mashed potatoes. Garnish with sliced *green onions*.

Roulade of Uku and 'Ahi

tomato - ogo salad

Serves 4

4	each	Uku Filets, 3.5 oz. each
4	each	'Ahi Filets, 2 oz. each
2	sheets	Nori (sushi quality)
1/2	gallon	Water
		Salt & Pepper to taste

Tomato - Ogo Salad -

1	each	Ripe Tomato (diced small)
1/2	each	Maui Onion or Red Onion (chopped)
1/4	cup	Green Onion (diced)
1/2	cup	Ogo (blanched and chopped)
2	Tbsp	Chili Pepper Water or Tabasco Sauce
1	tsp	Soy sauce
1	tsp	Ginger (grated)
1/2	tsp	Garlic (minced)
1/2	tsp	Olive Oil (extra virgin)
1	tsp	Champagne Vinegar
		Salt & Pepper to taste
		Parsley for garnish

Method -

Butterfly *uku* filets and pound flat with a meat tenderizer. Cut 'Ahi into 1 x 1 x 4 inch rectangular sections. Line *uku* filet with *nori* and place 'Ahi onto one side of the filet. Season with salt and pepper and roll. Wrap in clear food wrap making sure that the ends are nice and tight and waterproof. Place in boiling water for about 10 minutes. The 'Ahi in the *roulade* should be about medium rare to medium. Let rest for about 1 minute before slicing into medallions. Use a very sharp knife.

Tomato - Ogo Salad -

Combine all ingredients and season with salt and pepper.

To Serve -

Arrange medallions on a plate in a circle and top with Tomato - Ogo Salad. Garnish with parsley or other greenery.

Chilled Poached Salmon
gazpacho sauce with plain yogurt

Serves 6

6	each	Salmon Filets (skinless, 5 oz. each)
1	cup	White Wine
1	cup	Fish Stock
1	Tbsp	Champagne Vinegar
1	tsp	Fennel Seeds
3/4	cup	*Mirepoix* (carrots, onions, celery and leeks)

Gazpacho Sauce -

1/4	cup	Cucumbers (skinned and seeded, coarsely chopped)
1/4	cup	Zucchini (skinned, coarsely chopped)
1/4	cup	Red Onions (coarsely chopped)
1	each	Garlic Clove
1-1/2	cup	Tomato Juice
1/4	cup	Tomato (skinned and seeded, quartered)
1	tsp	Lemon (juice)
1/4	cup	Extra Virgin Olive Oil
		Worchestershire Sauce to taste
		Tabasco Sauce to taste
		Salt

Toppings -

6	Tbsp	Plain Yogurt
		Dill Sprigs

Gazpacho Sauce -

In a blender, add tomato juice and tomatoes. Purée until smooth. Add cucumbers, zucchini, onions, garlic, olive oil and lemon juice. Blend at low speed until vegetables are at a salsa consistency. Season with tabasco sauce, worchestershire sauce, salt and pepper. Refrigerate.

Fish Preparation -

In a large skillet or sautoir, add the fish stock, white wine, fennel seeds, champagne vinegar, and *mirepoix*. Bring to a boil then turn to a low simmer. Add salmon filets and cover. Simmer slowly for about 10 minutes. Remove and refrigerate.

To serve -

Ladle about 3 oz. of gazpacho on a plate and place chilled salmon in the center. Top with a tablespoon of yogurt atop each salmon filet and garnish with a sprig of dill. Steamed broccoli, new potatoes or green beans are a good accompaniment with this dish.

Lacquered Salmon

Serves 6

6	each	Salmon Filets (6-1/2 oz. each)
2	Tbsp	Sugar (granulated)
1-1/2	Tbsp	*Soy Sauce*
1	Tbsp	Peanut Oil
		Salt & Pepper to taste

Method -

Rub filets with *soy sauce* and lightly coat one side with sugar.

Heat pan, then add oil. Place salmon filet with the sugar side down in pan. Sear until golden brown and turn. Cook until done. Serve with your favorite sauce or with a lemon.

Pan Seared Salmon
chinese black bean lime sauce

Serves 4

4	each	Salmon Filets (6-1/2 oz. each)
1	Tbsp	Black Beans (salted)
1/2	tsp	Clove Garlic (peeled and finely chopped)
1/4	cup	White Wine
1	each	Lime (juice of medium sized)
1/2	tsp	*Soy Sauce*
1/2	tsp	*Oyster Sauce*
1/4	cup	Heavy Cream
3/4	cup	Butter (soft)
2	Tbsp	Oil
		Salt & Pepper to taste
		Green Onions (julienne) for garnish

Chinese Black Bean Lime Sauce -

Put black beans, garlic, *ginger*, white wine, lime juice, *oyster sauce*, and *soy sauce* in a sauce pot and simmer for about 3 minutes. Add heavy cream and simmer until mixture thickens. Turn stove down to low and add butter slowly, whipping constantly. Season with salt and pepper.

Salmon -

Heat frying pan on stove until pan is hot. Add 1 ounce of oil. Place salmon in pan and sear until brown on one side. Turn and sear until done.

To serve -

Place salmon on a plate and lace with the sauce. (*Cake noodles* and a Chinese vegetable make a good accompaniment to the dish.) Garnish dish with julienne of *green onions*.

I thought of a local-style Chinese black bean sauce,
but I didn't want it in exactly that presentation.
Instead, I created a beurre blanc sauce and placed the
salmon on a cake noodle that we created.

Cornmeal Crusted Medallion of Salmon
whole grain mustard sauce

Serves 4

8	each	Salmon Filets (3 oz. each)
1	cup	Cornmeal (fine)
1/2	cup	Olive Oil
3	Tbsp	Whole Grain Mustard
1/4	cup	White Wine
1/4	cup	Rice Wine Vinegar
1	tsp	*Green Onions* (chopped)
1/4	cup	Heavy Cream
2	tsp	Dill (chopped)
1/2	cup	Butter
		Dill Sprig (to garnish)
		Salt & Pepper to taste

Method -

Place the corn meal in a bowl. Season salmon with salt and pepper and press firmly into the cornmeal. Heat pan until very hot then add oil. Sauté salmon filets until golden brown on one side. Turn and cook salmon to desired doneness.

Sauce -

In a small sauce pot on medium heat, add white wine, vinegar, mustard, *green onions* and dill. Reduce mixture by half. Add heavy cream and reduce until cream is thick. Turn down the heat to low. Whisk in butter mixture a little at a time until all the butter is incorporated. Season with salt and pepper. Strain through a fine sieve. Set aside until needed and keep warm.

To serve -

Ladle about 2 oz. of sauce onto plate. Place two medallions of salmon on top of sauce. Garnish with a sprig of dill. Serve with steamed new potatoes and fresh kernels of corn.

Pan Seared Filet of Salmon

fennel, spinach & champagne butter sauce

Serves 4

4	each	Salmon Filets (6 oz. each with skin on)
2	Tbsp	Olive Oil (for searing fish)
1/2	cup	Fennel (thinly sliced)
1/4	tsp	Garlic (chopped)
1/2	lb	Spinach (cleaned and stemmed)
1	Tbsp	Fresh Basil (shredded)
1	Tbsp	Whole Butter or Olive Oil
2	cups	Mashed Potatoes (cooked)
1	cup	Champagne Butter Sauce (recipe to follow)
		Salt & Pepper to taste

Champagne Butter Sauce -

1/2	tsp	*Green Onions* (chopped)
1/4	cup	Champagne
1/4	cup	White Vinegar
1/4	tsp	Cracked Black Pepper
1/2	cup	Heavy Cream
1/2	cup	Whole Butter
		Salt & Pepper to taste

Method -

Heat a large skillet over medium heat and add 1 tablespoon olive oil. Season the fish with salt and pepper and place in the heated pan with the skin side up. Continue to cook in the pan until the salmon is well seared and turn the filets using a spatula, being careful not to tear the fish. Continue to cook the fish for 2 to 3 minutes and remove from pan.

Lower the heat in the pan and add the butter or olive oil. Add in the fennel and garlic and sauté until soft. Add the spinach and basil and continue to cook until soft. Season with salt and pepper to taste.

Champagne Butter Sauce -

In a small saucepan, heat the *green onions*, champagne, vinegar and pepper to a boil. Reduce by half and add the cream. Reduce by half and lower the heat. Slowly whip in the butter so that it emulsifies. Strain and season with salt and pepper.

To Plate -

Spoon a portion of mashed potatoes in the middle of the plate. Place the fish on top and spoon the fennel mixture around the fish. Drizzle with the Champagne-Butter Sauce. Garnish with a sprig of the fennel top or dill.

Pan Fried Potato Crusted Salmon
wild mushroom and spinach broth

Serves 4

4	each	Salmon Filets (6 oz. each)
2	each	Baker Potato (medium)
1	cup	Wild Mushrooms (Porcini, Chanterelles, Shiitakes, Morels, etc.)
1/2	cup	Button Mushrooms
14	leaves	Spinach (cleaned & stemmed)
3	cups	Veal Stock
3	Tbsp	Salad Oil
1/4	cup	Bacon (finely diced)
1	each	Tomato (seeded & diced)
1	each	Garlic Clove (coarsely chopped)
1	Tbsp	*Green Onions* (chopped)
1/4	cup	White Wine
2	Tbsp	Butter
		Salt & Pepper to taste

Method -

Peel potato and put through a vegetable noodle machine. Blanch potato noodles in hot water for about 4 minutes. Cool immediately with ice water. Drain salmon and season with salt and pepper then wrap salmon with potatoes.

Sauté bacon in sauce pan over medium heat until medium cooked. Add *green onions* and garlic and sauté for a minute. Add mushrooms and cook for about 5 minutes. Add stock and simmer until stock reduces down by half. Add spinach and tomato. Simmer for another 2 minutes and add butter. Season with salt and pepper.

Heat frying pan then add a little oil. Add potato crusted salmon and sauté until golden brown on one side and turn. Cook until golden brown. Ladle sauce on the bottom of the plate and place cooked salmon on sauce.

Tofu & Shrimp Napoleon

Serves 4

Tofu -

1	block	Firm Tofu
8	each	Large Shrimp
2	cups	Peanut Oil
1/2	cup	Flour
2	each	Eggs (beaten)
2	cups	*Panko* or Fresh Bread Crumbs

Sauce -

3/4	cup	Chicken Stock
2	Tbsp	*Soy Sauce*
1	tsp	Chili Sauce
1/4	cup	Peanut Butter
1/2	cup	Coconut Milk
1	Tbsp	Cornstarch
1	Tbsp	Cold Water
1/4	cup	Chopped Peanuts (for garnish)
		Green Onions (for garnish)
		Black Sesame Seeds (for garnish)

Method -

Cut tofu into 2-inch squares, 3/8 inch thick (8 pieces). Carefully flour each square then dip into egg. Roll into *panko* and reserve on the side.

Peel and devein shrimp.

In a medium-sized sauce pot, heat chicken stock, *soy sauce* and chili sauce to a simmer. Add cornstarch mixed with equal parts of cold water. Simmer 3 to 4 minutes. Stir in peanut butter and mix until smooth. Whisk in coconut milk and season with salt and pepper. Keep warm.

In a large frying pan add peanut oil until half deep and pre-heat oil to 350 degrees F. Place tofu square in pan and fry until golden brown (1-1/2 minutes). Turn over and cook about 1 more minute. Remove and place on paper towel to drain off excess oil.

While tofu is cooking, shrimp can be grilled, baked or sautéed. Place small amount of sauce in the center of the plate. Place 1 square of tofu on top of sauce then top with 1 shrimp. Ladle a small amount of sauce on top. Repeat process.

Garnish with chopped peanuts, *green onions* and black sesame seeds.

Fried Stuffed Eggplant with Tofu and Crabmeat
gingered dashi

Serves 6

1	block	Tofu
1/2	cup	Crabmeat
1/2	tsp	Garlic (chopped)
1/4	tsp	*Ginger* (chopped)
3	each	Japanese Eggplant
2	cups	*Panko* or Fresh Bread Crumbs
1-1/2	cups	Flour
1	each	Egg
1/4	cup	Water
2	cups	Salad Oil (for frying)

Gingered Dashi -

1	piece	*Dashi Konbu* (seaweed- 4 inches)
1/2	cup	*Bonito Flakes*
1	tsp	*Ginger* (grated)
1-1/2	Tbsp	*Soy Sauce*
3-1/2	cups	Water
		Mirin (to taste)
1/8	cup	*Bonito Flakes*

Method -

Slice eggplant into thin slices lengthwise. Line on a sheet pan. Season with salt and pepper. Bake in oven at 325 degrees F. for about 8 minutes. Remove and cool.

Break tofu up into little bits by using the back of a spoon or fork. Mix in crabmeat, garlic and *ginger*. Season with salt and pepper.

Line eggplant slices in a row on a cutting board. Put one small scoop of tofu mixture at one end of each eggplant. Roll into a ball. Freeze for about half an hour. Remove and coat lightly with flour.

In a bowl, add egg, water and flour and mix until smooth (about the consistency of pancake batter). Dip eggplant into batter and roll in *panko*. Pan fry and serve immediately.

Gingered Dashi -

Boil water and *dashi konbu* for about 10 to 15 minutes. Remove konbu and add 1/2 cup *bonito flakes*. Let simmer for about 3 to 4 minutes. Remove and strain. Add 1/8 cup *bonito flakes* and let sit for about 10 minutes. Strain into another pot. Add *soy sauce, mirin* and *ginger*. Simmer for about 3 minutes until the flavor of *ginger* is present. Season with salt and pepper.

To Serve -

Ladle about 3 to 4 ounces of *dashi* into a soup dish. Place two fried eggplant onto *dashi*. Garnish with julienne of *green onions*.

Gingered Crabmeat & Tobiko Caviar Napoleon

Serves 6

6	oz.	Dungeness Crab Meat
2	Tbsp	*Tobiko* Caviar
1/8	cup	*Green Onions* (diced)
2	Tbsp	Mayonnaise
1	tsp	*Ginger* (grated fine)
6	each	Won Ton Pi (cut into eighths)
2	tsp	Black Sesame Seeds (for garnish)
2	pieces	*Green Onions* (for garnish)
		Salt & Pepper to taste

Method -

In a stainless steel bowl, combine all of the ingredients except the won tons. Season with salt and pepper. Let rest for about half an hour for the flavors to develop. Fry *won ton pi* in pre-heated oil (350 degrees F.) until golden brown. Be sure to turn the *won ton pi* over so both sides are nice and brown.

Spoon crab mixture onto the center of one *won ton pi*. Place another *won ton pi* on top and add crab mixture. Top with another piece of *won ton pi* and garnish with *green onions* and black sesame seeds.

*I like to work with seafood, because I believe
there's a lot more versatility to it than meat.
The only thing you can really change
about meat is the sauce.*

Saffron Risotto with Shrimp and Scallop

lemon tomato butter sauce

Serves 4

12	each	Shrimp (21-25 count, peeled and deveined with the tail left on)
12	each	Scallops (20-30 count)
1-1/2 cups		Arborio Rice (Italian Rice)
3-4 cups		Clam or Fish Stock
1/4 tsp		Saffron
1	tsp	*Green Onions*
1/2 each		Medium Onion
1	Tbsp	Parmesan Cheese (grated fine)
1/2 cup		White Wine
2	Tbsp	Butter
1	Tbsp	Olive Oil
		Salt & Pepper to taste

Method -

Sauté *green onions* and onion with olive oil. Add saffron and white wine and reduce by half.

Add rice and cook for about 2 minutes, stirring constantly so rice will not burn. Add stock and simmer for about 16 minutes, stirring once in a while. Rice should be al dente and not mushy.

Add shrimp and scallops after 13 minutes of cooking the rice. Stir in butter and cheese and season with salt and pepper.

For a different flavor, you can sear seafood first before adding it to the risotto.

Pan Fried Shrimp

chinese salsa

Serves 6

24	each	Shrimp (16 - 20 count, peeled and deveined)
6	each	Skewers (bamboo or metal)
1	clove	Garlic
1/4	cup	*Soy Sauce*
1/8	cup	Vegetable Oil
1/4	tsp	Sesame Oil
1/2	tsp	*Ginger* (chopped)

Chinese Salsa -

6 - 8	each	Black Mushrooms (diced)
4	each	Tomato (medium)
1/2	cup	*Green Onion* (chopped)
1/4	cup	*Chinese Parsley* (chopped)
2	cloves	Garlic (minced)
1	Tbsp	*Ginger* (diced fine)
3	Tbsp	Red Wine Vinegar
2	Tbsp	Sesame Oil
1	Tbsp	Oil
1/2	tsp	Sugar
1	tsp	Chinese Chili Sauce
1/2	tsp	Salt
		Chinese Parsley or *Green onion* (for garnish)

Method -

Combine *soy sauce*, vegetable oil, sesame oil, garlic and *ginger*. Mix well. Add shrimp and marinate for about 2 hours. Place 4 shrimps on each skewer.

Chinese Salsa -

Mix all ingredients and chill for about 5 hours.

Pan fry marinated shrimp. Serve with salsa and garnish with *Chinese parsley* or *green onions*.

Won Ton Wrapped Shrimp
thai curry sauce

Serves 4

16	each	Shrimp (16-20 or 21-25 count, peeled and deveined)
16	each	*Won Ton Pi* (pasta sheets)
1	Tbsp	Thai Red Curry
1	cup	Coconut Milk (canned)
2	inch	*Lemon Grass*
7	leaves	Thai Basil
1/2	each	Cinnamon Stick
3	each	Whole Cloves
1/2	cup	Whipping Cream
1	inch	*Ginger*
1/2	cup	White Wine
1/4	tsp	*Fish Sauce*
3	each	Lime Leaf (optional)
1	quart	Salad Oil
1/4	cup	Cornstarch

Method -

Wrap shrimp with *won ton pi*. Moisten corner of *won ton pi* with water to adhere. Sprinkle pan with cornstarch and lay wrapped shrimp on pan. Set aside until needed.

In a sauce pot, add the white wine, cinnamon stick, cloves, *ginger*, *lemon grass*, and curry. Reduce by half and add coconut milk and whipping cream.

Add basil, *fish sauce* and lime leaf and simmer for about 20 minutes. Season with salt and pepper. Strain and keep warm.

In another pot, heat oil until 350 degrees F. Fry shrimp for about 1-1/2 minutes. Remove and coat with sauce. Serve immediately.

It's simple; it's tasty; it's easy to make.
You can use a sauce or not use a sauce.
The pancetta should be cut while in a frozen
state, so it can be cut thin.
It's great because it's salt-cured, but not
smoked like American bacon, so it doesn't
take any flavor away from the shrimp . . .

Pancetta Wrapped Shrimp
roasted red pepper aioli

Serves 4

16	each	Shrimp (21-25 count, peeled and deveined with the tail left on)
16	slices	*Pancetta* or Gourmet Smoked Bacon (sliced 1/16 inch thick)
		Chinese Parsley (for garnish)
		Salt & Pepper to taste

Roasted Red Pepper Aioli -

1	each	Red Bell Pepper
1	each	Egg Yolk
1/4	tsp	Garlic (chopped)
1/2	cup	Vegetable Oil
		Salt & Pepper to taste

Method -

Season shrimp with salt and pepper. Wrap each shrimp (width-wise) with *pancetta*, starting from the head end of the shrimp, and making sure to overlap each layer. Bring a sauté pan to medium heat and fry the shrimp until each side is rendered and crispy. When this is completed, the shrimp will be cooked. Transfer the shrimp onto an absorbent paper and drain.

Roasted Red Pepper Aioli -

Over an open flame or under a broiler, roast the pepper, turning occasionally until all sides are charred. Place the pepper on a plate and cover with plastic wrap until cool. Rub off with hands the charred skin and remove the stem, seeds and ribs. Chop until fine and set aside. Wisk in the yolk and garlic in a small *non-reactive* bowl using a small wire whip.

Slowly drizzle in the oil until it becomes thick (The oil will emulsify with the yolk, giving it a mayonnaise-like consistency.) Add in the chopped pepper and season with salt and pepper.

Place shrimp on a serving plate. Spoon a dollop of the Roasted Red Pepper *Aioli* and garnish with parsley.

We wanted to do a traditional Hawaiian dish,
but something more healthy, without the pork, beef, and
all the fats and oils . . .

Ti Leaf Steamed Seafood
lemon tomato butter sauce

Serves 4

Seafood -

8	each	Large *ti* leaves (cleaned)
12	oz.	'Opakapaka (cut into 1 inch squares)
20	each	Scallops
12	pieces	Shrimp 21-25 count (peeled and deveined)
4	each	Roma tomatoes (diced large)
1-1/2	cup	Button mushrooms (sliced)
1	cup	Basil (destemmed loosely packed)
2	bunch	Spinach (cleaned and destemmed)
		Butcher's Twine
		Salt & Pepper to taste

Lemon Tomato Butter Sauce -

1	Tbsp	*Green Onions* (chopped)
1/4	cup	Rice vinegar
1/4	cup	White wine
1/4	cup	Heavy cream
1	cup	Butter (cut into small pieces)
2	Each	Roma tomatoes (diced small with seeds removed)
1/8	cup	*Green Onions* (diced)
2	Tbsp	Red onions (diced small)
1	each	Juice of one lemon
2	cups	Butter
		Salt & Pepper to taste

Method -

On a large work area, place the ti leaves in a "T" pattern. Toss together the spinach and basil and divide into 8 portions. Place one portion of spinach into the center of the ti leaf. In a large bowl, toss fish with salt and pepper to taste. Place equal amounts of fish on top of spinach. Toss shrimp and scallops in separate bowls with salt and pepper.

In the center of the spinach, place 3 shrimps and 5 scallops. Top with tomato and mushrooms. Divide the remainder of the spinach to cover the seafood. Pick up the four stems and tie tightly with butcher's twine. Steam in a steamer or double boiler until done. Approximately 20 minutes.

Lemon Tomato Butter Sauce -

In a small bowl, toss *green onions*, tomatoes and red onions. Reserve. In a sauce pan, add the *green onions*, rice vinegar and white wine. Reduce by half and add the cream. Reduce until half or until cream thickens. Reduce heat and add butter slowly, whisking constantly until smooth. Remove from heat and season with salt and pepper. Strain with a fine sieve. Add diced *green onions*, tomatoes and red onions. Reserve in a warm area of the kitchen.

To serve -

Place *ti* leaf bundle in the middle of the plate. Cut strings and fold the stems under the bundle. Drizzle the sauce lightly over the seafood and garnish with shaved onions.

Grilled Swordfish, Kiwi Pineapple Salsa
lime butter sauce

Serves 6

6	each	Swordfish Steaks, (6 1/2 oz. each)

Salsa -

3	each	Kiwi (peeled and diced)
3/4	cup	Pineapple (diced)
1/4	tsp	Jalapeno (finely diced)
1	Tbsp	*Chinese parsley* (chopped)
1/2	tsp	Oregano (chopped)
1/4	tsp	*Cumin* (ground)
1/4	tsp	Garlic (chopped)
2	tsp	Lime (juice)
		Salt & Pepper to taste

Lime Butter Sauce -

1/2	cup	White Wine
1/4	cup	Rice Wine Vinegar
1	Tbsp	*Green Onions* (minced)
1/4	cup	Heavy Cream
1	cup	Butter (cut into 1 oz. cubes)
1	tsp	Lime (*zest*)
1	each	Lime (juice)
		Salt & Pepper to taste

Salsa -

In a medium mixing bowl, combine all ingredients and season with salt and pepper. Keep chilled until service.

Lime Butter Sauce -

In a small sauce pan on medium heat, add white wine, rice wine vinegar, *green onions*, lime juice and lime *zest*. Reduce by half. Add heavy cream and reduce by half. Whisk in the softened butter a cube at a time, stirring constantly. Strain through a fine sieve then season with salt and pepper.

To serve -

Grill swordfish. Ladle 1 oz. of sauce on the plate. Place swordfish on top of sauce and top with the Kiwi-Pineapple Salsa.

*People like kiwi fruit. They can relate to
kiwi and the colors of the kiwi combined
well with pineapple—
it was a great presentation . . .
and the flavors worked well together, too . . .*

Pan Fried Sea Scallops
roast kumquat relish & champagne sauce

Serves 4

12	each	Scallops (21-25 count)
1	Tbsp	Olive Oil

Champagne Sauce -

1/2 cup		Champagne
1/4 cup		Rice Wine Vinegar
1/4 cup		Heavy Cream
1 cup		Butter
1 tsp		Chopped Shallots

Kumquat Relish -

8	each	Fresh Kumquats
1/8 cup		Sugar
1/2 tsp		Grated Ginger
1 tsp		*Green Onions* (diced fine)

Scallops -

Heat frying pan then add oil. Sear the scallops in the pan, turning when golden brown. Remove when both sides are brown, approximately 2 to 3 minutes. Scallops should be a little underdone.

Champagne Sauce -

In a sauce pan, add champagne, rice wine vinegar, and shallots. Reduce to half. Add heavy cream and reduce by half. Add softened butter to mixture, a little at a time. Stir constantly. Strain through a sieve and season with salt and pepper.

Kumquat Relish -

In a bowl, toss together sugar and kumquats. Place in a non-stick pan and roast in a pre-heated oven at 350 degrees until sugar caramelizes (about 10 minutes). Remove and cool.

When kumquats are cool, slice into thin rings. Remove any seeds. Add ginger and *green onion*. Refrigerate until ready to use.

To Serve -

Ladle about 1-1/2 oz. of champagne sauce on a plate, place scallops in sauce. Top with the Roasted Kumquat Relish.

The tartness of the roasted kumquat fused together with the delicateness of the scallops gives it a light, almost lime-like flavor, kind of like a hide-and-seek effect . . .

Ballotine of Chicken Breast
caramelized maui onion sauce

Serves 4

4	each	Chicken Breast (skinless & all fat trimmed)
1/2	bunch	Spinach (slightly blanched)
1/2	each	Round Onion (julienne)
1	each	Carrot (small, julienne)
1	stalk	Celery (julienne)
1	Tbsp	Basil (chopped)
1/4	tsp	Black Pepper (fresh)

Mushroom Duxelle -

1	lb	Mushrooms (chopped in a food processor)
1/2	each	Yellow Onion (chopped in a food processor)
1	Tbsp	Garlic (chopped)
1/8	tsp	Rosemary (chopped)
1	Tbsp	Olive Oil

Caramelized Maui Onion Sauce -

1/2	cup	Maui Onions (julienne)
1	tsp	Garlic (chopped)
6	Tbsp	White Wine
2	Tbsp	Rice Wine Vinegar
2	Tbsp	Lite Soy Sauce
1	Tbsp	Basil (chopped)
1	cup	Chicken Stock
1	Tbsp	Olive Oil

Duxelle Preparation -

In a non-stick sauce pan, heat oil and sauté garlic and onions. Add mushrooms and rosemary and cook on medium heat until mixture is dry. Cool. Set aside until needed.

Chicken Preparation -

On a doubled piece of plastic food wrap, lay out one chicken breast. Top with another piece of food wrap. Pound the chicken with a mallet or a heavy pan to 3/8 inch thickness. Remove plastic wrap and season chicken with black pepper.

Lay out spinach to cover breast. Spread duxelle thinly over spinach. Place julienne vegetables in middle. Roll up breast and wrap tightly in double piece of food wrap. Tie ends so it becomes water tight.

Immerse in boiling water or chicken stock and simmer for about 12 minutes. Remove from pot and let cool for about 1 minute. Remove food wrap and slice. Serve over sauce.

Sauce Preparation -

In a sauce pan, heat 1 tablespoon olive oil and sauté maui onions and garlic. Sauté until slightly brown. Add white wine, rice wine vinegar and *soy sauce* while scraping bottom of pan lightly (deglazing). Add chicken stock and basil. Bring to a boil, lower heat to a simmer and reduce sauce by half. Season with salt and pepper and ladle sauce under chicken slices.

Grilled Breast of Chicken
chinese ratatouille

Serves 6

6	each	Chicken Breast (boneless)
1	bunch	*Chinese Parsley*
1	inch	*Ginger* Root
1	Tbsp	Soy Sauce
3	Tbsp	Water
1/2	tsp	Five Spice Seasoning

Vegetable Mix-

1/4	cup	Zucchini (medium diced)
1/4	cup	Red Bell Pepper (medium diced)
1/4	cup	Green Bell Pepper (medium diced)
1/4	cup	Red Onion (medium diced)
1/4	cup	Eggplant (medium diced)
1/4	cup	Roma Tomatoes (diced)
1	Tbsp	*Soy Sauce*
1-1/4	Tbsp	*Hoisin* Sauce
1	tsp	Garlic (minced)
1	Tbsp	Peanut Oil
		Salt & Pepper to taste

Method -

In a stainless steel bowl, add *Chinese parsley* and *ginger* root. Mash together with the bottom of a meat tenderizer. Add *five spice*, 1 tablespoon of *soy sauce* and water, then mix. Add chicken breasts and marinate for 4 hours. Grill over charcoal with skin side down first.

Vegetables -

Sauté vegetables in peanut oil. Add *hoisin* sauce, 1 tablespoon of *soy sauce* and garlic. Season with salt and pepper. Serve with chicken.

Macadamia Nut Breaded Chicken
guava lime sauce

Serves 6

6	each	Chicken Breast (boneless, skinless)
1/2	cup	*Macadamia Nuts* (chopped fine)
2	cups	*Panko* or Fresh Bread Crumbs
2	cups	Flour
2	cups	Water
1/2	cup	Flour
		Salt & Pepper to taste
1/4	cup	Oil

Guava Lime Sauce -

3/4	cup	*Guava* Purée
3/4	cup	Heavy Cream
1	each	Lime (juice)
1/4	cup	White Wine
1	cup	Butter (unsweetened)

Method -

In a bowl, mix together 2 cups flour and water until smooth with the consistency of pancake batter. Season chicken breast with salt and pepper. Lightly dust with flour. Dip breast in batter and roll into the *panko* mixture (*panko* and *macadamia nuts*). Reserve in the refrigerator until serving time.

Guava Lime Sauce -

In a sauce pot, add *guava* purée, lime juice and white wine. Reduce by half. Add heavy cream and reduce again by half. Whisk in butter a little at a time, stirring constantly. Be sure the heat is on low. As soon as all the butter is incorporated, remove from stove and season with salt and pepper. Strain through a fine sieve. Keep in a warm area.

Fry the chicken breast in enough oil to coat the bottom of the skillet. Fry until golden brown and flip. Cook through until done. Serve with *Guava* Lime Sauce on the side or on the bottom of the plate before placing chicken breast.

Chicken & Portuguese Sausage Cassoulet

Serves 6

6	each	Chicken Thighs (bone in)
1	lb	White Beans (soaked overnight)
1	lb	*Portuguese Sausage* (sliced 1/2 inch thick)
6	slices	Bacon
2	Tbsp	Olive Oil
1	lg.	Yellow Onion (diced large)
2	lg.	Carrots (diced large)
4	each	Garlic (chopped)
3	each	Bay Leaf
1	cup	White Vermouth or Dry White Wine
3	Tbsp	Fresh Thyme (or 1-1/2 tablespoon dry)
	Pinch	Allspice
6	Tbsp	Tomato Paste
5	cups	Beef or Chicken Stock
1	cup	Seasoned Bread Crumbs
		Salt & Pepper to taste

Method -

Sauté bacon strips in a large heavy bottom skillet or stock pot until crisp. Remove bacon and set aside until needed.

Add olive oil to bacon fat and sear chicken thighs. Remove and set aside.

Reduce heat to medium and add onions and garlic. Cook until translucent.

Deglaze with vermouth or white wine and reduce by half. Add tomato paste and stock. Add thyme, allspice, bay leaf, salt and pepper. Drain beans and add. Bring to a boil then reduce to a simmer for 20 minutes. Add chicken, sausage, bacon and carrots. Simmer for about 25 minutes more. Adjust seasoning.

Spoon into bowls and top with bread crumbs.

Chicken Wellington

Serves 4

4	each	Chicken Breasts (1/2 boneless, skinless)
12	each	Spinach Leaves (cleaned and washed)
4	each	Puff Pastry Sheets (cut in half)
1	each	Egg (beaten)
		Salt & Pepper to taste

Mushroom Duxelle -

1-1/2 cup		Button Mushrooms
1/2 cup		Ham (ground or finely diced)
1/8 cup		Onion (ground or finely diced)
2	Tbsp	Butter (clarified)
1/8 tsp		Rosemary
	Pinch	Fresh Thyme
1/2 cup		Heavy Cream
1/8 cup		*Panko* or Fresh Bread Crumbs
		Salt & Pepper to taste

Method -

Season chicken breast with salt and pepper. Brown in a skillet with butter or oil until chicken is half cooked. Let cool. Lay out one sheet of puff pastry. Line the center with spinach. Top with the chicken breast and then the duxelle. Fold puff pastry ends over and seal with beaten egg.

Place folded end side down on a cookie or baking sheet. Brush the top with the egg. Bake in pre-heated oven at 375 degrees F. until golden brown (about 12 minutes).

Mushroom Duxelle -

Lightly sauté onions and ham in clarified butter, until translucent. Add mushrooms and sauté lightly until water comes out. Turn down flame and reduce the liquid. When the liquid has been reduced, add cream, rosemary and thyme. Lightly reduce the cream until almost all is reduced. Add *panko* or bread crumbs and stir until it binds together. Season with salt and pepper. Cool before serving.

*Taste in food is a lot like tasting wine.
When you drink wine, you have to consider the "front", the "back", the "middle,"
the "finish"... everything.
You want your food to have that same
effect. You want someone to taste your food
and immediately go, "Wow! That's good!"
We'll work on a dish until we feel we've
achieved the "Wow! Effect."*

Chicken Napoleon
roasted pepper and soy jus

Serves 4

4	each	Chicken Breast
1	Tbsp	Vietnamese Chili Sauce
2	Tbsp	Vegetable Oil
1	each	Lime (juice)
1	tsp	Lime (*zest*)
		Salt & Pepper to taste

Shiitake and Spinach Ragout -

1	bunch	Spinach (cleaned and destemmed)
1/4	lb	*Shiitake* Mushroom (destemmed and sliced)
1/2	cup	Heavy Cream
1	Tbsp	*Hoisin* Sauce
1	Tbsp	*Soy Sauce*
1/2	Tbsp	Vietnamese Chili Sauce
1/2	tsp	Garlic (minced)

Roasted Pepper Soy Jus -

1	tsp	Vegetable Oil
1	each	Pepper (peeled, seeded and diced)
1	tsp	Garlic (chopped)
1	Tbsp	*Green Onions* (chopped)
1/4	cup	White Wine
1/4	cup	*Soy Sauce*
1	cup	Demi Glacé, or Rich Stock
1/4	cup	Cream

In a medium sauce pot, mix the chili sauce, oil, juice and 1 teaspoon of rind. Toss the chicken in the chili mixture. Season with salt and pepper and grill over medium heat. Set aside until needed.

Shiitake and Spinach Ragout -

Combine the cream, *hoisin*, *soy sauce* and chili sauce in a small sauce pot over medium heat and reduce by half. In a sauté pan, sauté the garlic until soft and add the mushrooms and spinach. Add the cream mixture to the mushroom and spinach and set aside.

Smoked Pepper Soy Jus -

Over a low fire, grill pepper over coals with a few kiawe or mesquite wood chips until the skin starts to blister. Try to keep it covered to intensify the smoke flavor. Wrap the pepper in plastic until cool. Rub off the skin and remove the stem, ribs and seeds.

In a medium sauce pan, heat the oil and sauté the garlic and *green onions* until translucent. Add the roasted pepper and sauté lightly. Deglaze with the *soy sauce* and white wine. Reduce by half and add the *demi glacé*. Bring to a simmer and cook for a few minutes to let the flavors come out.

To plate -

Spoon a 1/2 cup of mashed potatoes onto the middle of the plate. Place one half of a breast on the Soy Jus and spoon 1/4 cup of the *shiitake* mushroom and spinach mixture on top of the chicken. Top with the other half of breast and ladle more sauce on the breast. Serve.

Mexican Lasagna

Serves 12

3	cups	Ground Chicken
1-1/2 cups		Sour Cream
3	Tbsp	*Cumin* (ground)
2	Tbsp	Chili Powder
2	Tbsp	Oregano
		Salt & Pepper to taste
2	cups	*Green Onions* (diced)
8	cups	Monterey Jack Cheese (shredded)
18	each	Corn Tortillas (10 inch)
1	cup	Black Olives (sliced)
1	tsp	Vegetable Oil

Salsa -

3	cups	Tomatoes (diced)
2	Tbsp	*Chinese parsley* (chopped)
2	Tbsp	Garlic (chopped)
3	Tbsp	Onions (chopped)
1	Tbsp	Tabasco or Jalapeno Pepper (chopped)
		Salt & Pepper to taste

Salsa -

In a large mixing bowl, combine all ingredients together and let stand for about an hour for flavors to develop.

Chicken -

In a heated sauce pan, add a little oil and sauté ground chicken. Stir constantly to break up chicken into little balls. When fully cooked, drain excess oil. Add *cumin*, oregano, chili powder and sour cream. Season with salt and pepper.

Line a 12 inch x 18 inch cake pan with 6 corn tortillas – overlapping to cover bottom of pan. Top with half of the salsa mixture and half of the chicken mixture. Sprinkle 1/3 of cheese to cover. Spread olives evenly over the top and layer 6 more corn tortillas. Add the other half of the chicken mixture and 1/3 of the cheese and top with the last of the corn tortillas. Top with the other half of the salsa and cover the top with the remainder of the cheese and the chopped *green onions*.

Bake in a pre-heated oven for one hour at 325 degrees F. Let stand for 10 minutes to let hot mixture set before cutting.

Chicken Chili

with three beans

Serves 6

1	lb	Ground Chicken (skinless)
1/2	each	Round Onion (fine diced)
2	each	Ripe Steak Tomato (diced small)
2	cloves	Garlic (finely chopped)
1	cup	Tomatoes (crushed with juice)
3	Tbsp	Tomato Paste
3	Tbsp	Chili Powder
1	Tbsp	*Cumin* (ground)
1/2	tsp	Oregano
2	cans	Chicken Stock
1	Tbsp	Paprika
3	each	Bay Leaves
2	Tbsp	Salad Oil
1/4	cup	Cannelini Beans (dried)
1/4	cup	Cranberry Beans
1/4	cup	Pinto Beans
		Salt & Pepper to taste

Method -

Pre-soak beans separately for about 3 hours. Parboil beans until soft. Beans should be a little hard when bitten. Drain and cool.

In a deep skillet or sauce pot, sauté onions with salad oil for about 3 minutes. Add garlic and chicken and sauté until chicken is cooked. Add chili powder, paprika, tomato paste, *cumin*, oregano, and bay leaves. Mix thoroughly over medium heat. Add tomatoes, crushed tomatoes and chicken stock. Simmer for about 25 minutes. Add beans and simmer for another 25 minutes. Season with salt and pepper. For a spicier chili, add more chili powder or chopped jalapeno. Serve with rice or flour tortillas.

Smoked Chicken Pizza

One 10-inch Pizza

1	10-inch Pizza Dough
4 oz.	Smoked Chicken (shredded)
1/4 cup	Oven Dried Tomatoes
1/4 cup	Yellow Onions (sliced)
1/4 cup	*Shiitake* Mushrooms (sliced)
1/2 cup	Monterey Jack Cheese (grated)
1-1/2 Tbsp	*Hoisin* Sauce
1/ tsp	Sesame Oil
2 Tbsp	*Green Onion* (chopped)
1 Tbsp	*Chinese Parsley*

Pizza Dough -

1 pkg.	Instant Yeast
7/8 cup	Lukewarm Water
1-1/2 Tbsp	Salad Oil
3/4 tsp	Salt
2-2/3 cups	All Purpose Flour

Method -

Preheat oven to 425 degrees F. with the rack on the bottom 1/3 of the oven.

Sprinkle the smoked chicken, oven-dried tomatoes, onions and mushrooms evenly on the pizza dough. Sprinkle with the chopped *green onion* and *Chinese parsley*. Mix the *hoisin* and sesame oil and drizzle lightly over the pizza. Sprinkle evenly with the cheese. Bake for 12 minutes until the crust looks crisp and cooked. Serve.

Pizza Dough -

Dissolve the yeast in water. Let sit 5 minutes and add the oil, salt and all but 1/2 cup of the flour. Mix together. It should be soft but not sticky. To prevent stickiness, add more flour a little at a time. Place onto floured board and knead dough until smooth and it has an elastic-like consistency (but not sticky). Place in a lightly oiled bowl and let double in size.

Asian Style Roast Duckling
mango sauce

Serves 4

Duckling -

1	Duckling, 4 - 5 lb.
1/4 bunch	*Chinese parsley*
1/8 cup	*Green Onion* (chopped)
1/2-inch	*Ginger* (sliced)
1/2 tsp	*Five Spice* Seasoning
2 Tbsp	*Soy Sauce*
1/2 cup	White Vinegar
1 gallon	Water

Plum Glaze -

2 Tbsp	*Plum Sauce*
1 Tbsp	*Soy Sauce*
1 Tbsp	*Hoisin* Sauce
1 Tbsp	Honey
1/4 tsp	*Ginger* (chopped)
1/4 tsp	Fresh *Chinese Parsley* (chopped)
1/4 tsp	*Green Onion* (chopped)

Mango Sauce -

1/4 cup	Mango Purée
1/4 cup	Plum Wine
1 cup	*Demi Glacé* or rich Veal or Duck Stock
2 tsp	Butter
	Salt & Pepper to taste

To Prep Duckling -

In a large pot, bring 1 gallon of water to a boil. Add 1/2 cup white vinegar to the water. Trim any excess skin and fat from the duck. With a fork, prick holes in the breast and legs being careful not to stick the meat. Holding the duck over the water by the legs and using a large ladle, rinse the duck by pouring the boiling water over it. Continue to do this until the skin of the duck is very tight. In a small bowl using a mallet or pestle, smash the *Chinese parsley, green onion* and *ginger*. Mix in the *five spice, soy sauce* and water. Place the duck in the refrigerator for 24 hours to dry. This is best done by placing the duck on the top shelf and close to the fan. Roast in a pre-heated oven at 350 degrees F. oven for 1 hour and 15 minutes. In the last 15 minutes, brush with the plum glaze (recipe follows).

To serve, slice the thigh meat by holding onto the leg and carving down on the thigh. Transfer to a large serving tray. Slice the breast off by cutting down the middle of the breast bone and following the breast bone. Lay the breast on the cutting board and slice at an angle. Transfer to the serving platter. Remove the legs and place them in the middle. Garnish with fresh *Chinese parsley*.

Plum Glaze -

In a medium mixing bowl, combine all ingredients. Set aside until duck is ready for glazing.

Mango Sauce -

In a small sauce pan on medium heat, combine the mango purée and the plum wine. Bring to a simmer and reduce by half. Add the *demi glacé* and bring to a boil. Reduce to simmer and continue to cook for 3 to 5 minutes. Turn to low and whisk in the butter. Season with salt and pepper. Serve on the side with the duck.

In some Asian cooking, you don't have heavy sauces. Peoples' tastes are a little lighter, a little fresher...al dente'.

Grilled Marinated Breast of Chicken
salsa verde

Serves 6

Chicken -

6		Chicken Breast (skinless, 6 oz. each)
1	each	Lime (juice)
1	Tbsp	Fresh Sage (chopped)
1/2	tsp	Garlic (chopped)
1/4	cup	Canola Oil
1/2	tsp	*Chinese Parsley* (chopped)

Salsa Verde -

1	lb	Tomatillos (peeled, washed & quartered)
1	each	Green Chili (chopped)
1/8	cup	*Green Onions* (chopped)
1	Tbsp	*Chinese Parsley* (chopped)
1/3	tsp	Garlic (chopped)
1	Tbsp	Lime (juice)
		Oregano (whole leaf), to taste
		Cumin to taste
		Salt & Pepper to taste

Chicken -

Mix together lime juice, *Chinese parsley*, sage, oil, garlic, salt, and black pepper. Cut chicken breasts in half. Toss in marinade and refrigerate for about 4 hours. Remove and grill until done.

Salsa Verde -

In a blender, purée the tomatillos, green chili, *green onions*, *Chinese parsley*, garlic, lime juice, oregano, and *cumin*. Season with salt and pepper. More green chilis may be added to make it spicier. Serve sauce under chicken breast and garnish with *Chinese parsley*.

Pot Roast Jardinere

Serves 4

3	lb.	Boneless Chuck
3/4	cup	Carrots (diced medium)
3/4	cup	Celery (diced medium)
3/4	cup	Onion (diced medium)
1	quart	Beef Stock (to cover meat)
1	clove	Garlic (whole)
3	each	Bay Leaves
		Sprig of Thyme
2	Tbsp	Tomato Paste
1/4	cup	Butter (melted)
1/8	cup	All Purpose Flour
1	cup	Carrots, Onion and Celery (julienne and blanched)
2	Tbsp	Oil
2	Tbsp	Parsley (chopped) for garnish

Method -

Pre-heat a brazier or large pot big enough to sauté the meat. Add oil and sear meat until brown on all sides. Cover with beef stock. Add onions, celery, carrots, bay leaves, thyme and tomato paste. Stir until tomato paste is dissolved. When stock comes to a boil, cover and bake in a pre-heated oven set at 350 degrees F. for about 2 hours, or until meat is tender depending upon the size of the roast. Remove meat from pot and keep warm. Mix together flour and butter until smooth. Add flour mixture (beurre manie) to stock and whisk constantly until sauce thickens. Continue to simmer over low heat for about 20 minutes until the flour cooks and sauce is smooth. Strain and reserve on the side.

Slice meat and ladle gravy over. Garnish with blanched julienne of vegetables. Sprinkle with chopped parsley. Serve with steamed rice or mashed potatoes.

This is different—a real far-out dish—
to blend seafood and meat together.
People normally keep the two separate,
but I stuffed the veal with shrimp and
spinach, so when you cut it, it has
a nice color and look to it.

Roast Loin of Veal Stuffed with Prawns and Spinach

tarragon sauce

Serves 4

1-1/2 lbs.	Boneless Veal Loin (silver skin removed)	
8 pieces	Shrimp, 21 - 25 count (peeled and deveined)	
1/2 bunch	Spinach (cleaned and destemmed)	
	Salt & Pepper to taste	
	Butcher's Twine	

Tarragon Sauce -

Pan and Drippings from searing the loin

1/2 cup	Red Wine
1/2 tsp	Fresh Tarragon (chopped) or 1/4 tsp dried
1 cup	Demi Glacé or Rich Stock
2 Tbsp	Butter

In a pot of boiling water, blanch the shrimp until almost cooked. Remove from the water and cool shrimp in a bowl of ice water.

Lay the veal loin on a cutting board and make a cut the length of loin, parallel to the board about 3/4 of the way in. This will allow you to open up the loin like a book. With the loin still on the board, cover with plastic wrap and lightly pound out the loin so it will be 1/2 inch thick. Season with salt and pepper. Lay out the spinach along the length of the loin, covering 3/4's of the way across. (1/4 of veal meat should be exposed)

Lay the shrimp out by over lapping them on top of the spinach following the length of the loin. Cut the butcher's twine into lengths that will allow you to tie around the loin. You will need 4 pieces of twine. Tie the twine around the loin starting at one end. Do not tie too tight as you will force the shrimps to slip out.

Season the loin with salt and pepper. In a heavy skillet over medium heat with a small amount of oil, sear the loin evenly on all sides. Transfer the loin to a roasting pan, but save the skillet to make the sauce. Roast the loin in a pre-heated oven at 325 degrees F. for 20 minutes or until internal temperature reaches 120 degrees F. Spoon a small amount of sauce onto a plate. Slice the loin and place on the sauce.

Tarragon Sauce -

Heat the pan previously used to sear the veal loin over medium heat. Pour out any excess oil from the pan. Deglaze the pan with red wine. Add the tarragon. Reduce by half. Add the demi glacé and continue to simmer for 3 to 5 minutes. Remove from heat and whisk in the butter until smooth. Season with salt and pepper.

Tian of Lamb with Spinach and Mushroom
cabernet mint sauce

Serves 4

4		Boneless Lamb Loins (4 oz. each)
1	bunch	Spinach (cleaned and destemmed)
1	cup	Tomato (diced)
1/2 tsp		Garlic (minced)
4		Baking Potatoes
1/4 cup		Butter
		Salt & Pepper to taste
1		4 - 4 1/2 inch (diameter) Round Cookie Cutter or Aluminum Foil Ring

Cabernet Mint Sauce -

1/2 bunch Mint

3 Tbsp Sugar

1 cup Cabernet Sauvignon Wine

1/2 cup *Demi-Glacé* or Rich Gravy

2 tsp Butter

Bake the potatoes in a pre-heated oven at 350 degree F. until done (about 45 minutes). Set aside to cool. Slice potatoes into 1/4-inch slices.

Season the loins with salt and pepper. In a medium-sized skillet, sear the lamb loin on all sides. Transfer to a roasting pan and roast in a 350 degree F. oven for 15 minutes, or until it reaches an internal temperature of 120 degrees F. In the skillet, place half of the butter and pan fry the potato slices until golden brown. Keep warm on the side.

In a hot sauté pan, add the remaining butter and quickly stir fry the garlic, spinach and tomato. Keep warm on the side.

Place a ring in the middle of the plate. Fill halfway with the potatoes and finish filling with the spinach mixture. Press lightly on the top and remove ring.

Slice the loin thinly and lay out in a fan shape around the top of the spinach. Drizzle with the sauce.

Cabernet Mint Sauce -

Pick the mint leaves from the stem and place on cutting board. Sprinkle the sugar over the mint and chop together.

In a small sauce pot on medium heat, place the chopped mint and add the wine. Reduce by half the volume.

Add the demi-glacé and bring to a boil. Reduce heat and simmer and cook for 5 minutes.

Reduce heat to low and whisk in the butter. Season with salt and pepper.

Baked Ham
guava sherry sauce

Serves 16

1		Ham; scored, bone-in (optional: stud with cloves)
2	cups	Lemon Lime Soda
4	cups	*Guava* Nectar or Juice
1/2	cup	Sweet Sherry
1	each	Cinnamon Stick
3	each	Whole Cloves
1/4	cup	*Guava* Jelly
1	each	Lemon (juice)
3	Tbsp	Cornstarch
4	Tbsp	Water
		Salt & Pepper to taste

Baking -

Set studded ham in roasting pan and place in pre-heated oven with temperature set at 375 degrees F. for about 10 minutes. Lower temperature to 325 degrees F. At this time, combine 2 cups of lemon lime soda with one cup *guava* nectar. Remove and baste generously with the mixture. Return ham back to oven. Baste every 15 minutes until mixture is gone. Depending on the size of the ham, allow 10 minutes per pound. After mixture is gone, baste with the juices of the ham in the roasting pan.

Guava Sherry Sauce -

In a sauce pot, combine the balance of the *guava* juice with sherry, cinnamon stick, cloves, *guava* jelly, lemon juice, and the drippings from the ham. Reduce until mixture is 3/4 original volume. Season and thicken with cornstarch and water mixture. Strain and serve.

Note: Fresh *guavas* can be substituted for the juice. To use fresh *guava*, pare skin and blend pulp in blender until smooth. Strain through a sieve. Fresh *guava* juice is not as sweet as the prepared juice. Sugar, jelly, or honey can be added to sweeten sauce.

Roast Cornmeal Crusted Pork Loin
sweet corn barbecue sauce

Serves 6

Sauce -

2	cups	Beef Stock
1	Tbsp	Dijon Mustard
1/2	cup	Ketchup
1	tsp	Salt
1	tsp	*Cumin*
1/4	tsp	Cayenne
1/2	cup	Fresh Roasted Corn (cut off cob)
1	tsp	Oregano (fresh and chopped)
1	Tbsp	*Chinese Parsley* (fresh and chopped)
1	tsp	Garlic
1	Tbsp	Onion (chopped)
	Dash	Worchestershire Sauce

Pork Loin -

1	whole	Boneless Pork Loin (3-4 lbs.)
2	cups	Cornmeal
1/4	cup	Vegetable Oil
		Salt & Pepper to taste

Sweet Corn Barbecue Sauce -

Lightly sauté onion and garlic over medium high heat. Add remainder of the ingredients and simmer for about 10 minutes. Purée in blender and keep warm.

Pork Loin -

Season the pork loin with salt and pepper and roll in cornmeal. Heat skillet until hot. Add oil and sear pork loin on both sides.

Pre-heat oven to 350 degrees F. Roast pork loin for about 20 to 30 minutes.

To serve -

Ladle sauce on the bottom of the plate and place pork loin on sauce.

Sautéed Wai'anae Escargots in Puff Pastry

garlic sherry cream sauce

Serves 4

6	oz.	Wai'anae Escargots
1-1/2 cups		Button Mushrooms (quartered; fresh)
1	tsp	Garlic (chopped)
1	tsp	*Green Onions* (chopped)
1	tsp	Parsley (chopped)
1/4 cup		Dry Sherry
1	cup	Heavy Cream
2	Tbsp	Whole Butter (unsalted)
1/4 cup		Tomatoes (finely diced)
4	each	Baked Puff Pastry Squares (filo dough)

Roux -

1	tsp	Butter (melted)
1	tsp	All Purpose Flour

Method -

In a medium sauté pan, melt 1 tablespoon of the butter over medium heat. Add the garlic and *green onions* and sauté lightly until translucent. Add the mushrooms and sauté until soft.

Deglaze the pan with the sherry and reduce by half. Add the cream and bring to a simmer and reduce by half. In a small cup or bowl, mix the melted butter and flour to make a *roux*. When the cream has reduced, whisk in the *roux* and continue to simmer for 1 to 2 minutes. Add in the parsley and season with salt and pepper.

Add the escargots and the remaining 1 tablespoon butter and whisk until smooth. Adjust the seasoning and spoon into the pastry shells.

Puff Pastry Shell Preparation -

Using a frozen sheet of puff pastry, cut any shape you desire at least 3 x 3 inches. Cut a second piece following the outside of the puff pastry but a 1/4 inch from the original cut and only cutting halfway through the puff pastry. Brush the pastry with a beaten egg wash and bake in pre-heated oven at 425 degrees F. for 8 minutes. Cool and cut through the puff pastry to remove the inside of the pastry. Reserve this piece to use as a cover.

People in Hawai'i like lamb, and we
prepare it with a macadamia nut crust to
make it a little more Hawaiian.
Here again, you have a nice texture to it.
Also, the flavor of the macadamia nut,
when roasted, adds a nice, sweet
fragrant smell and taste.

Macadamia Nut Crusted Rack of Lamb
cabernet mint sauce

Serves 4

1		8-Bone Lamb Rack (frenched)
		Salt & Pepper to taste
2	Tbsp	Dijon Mustard
3/4	cup	*Panko*
1/4	cup	Macadamia Nuts (chopped)
1	tsp	Garlic (chopped)
1/4	cup	Butter (melted)
1	tsp	Olive Oil

Cabernet Mint Sauce -

1/2		bunch Mint
3	Tbsp	Sugar
1	cup	Cabernet Sauvignon Wine
1/2	cup	*Demi-Glacé* or Rich Gravy
2	tsp	Butter

Method -

Heat a small sauté pan over medium heat. Season the lamb rack with salt and pepper and sear the rack on all sides in the pan with a small amount of oil. Cool.

Brush the rack with the dijon mustard being sure to cover all of the meat area to ensure the crumbs will stick.

In a small mixing bowl, mix together the *panko*, macadamia nuts and garlic. Add the melted butter slowly while mixing, using just enough to make the crumbs moist.

Roast in a 375 degree F. pre-heated oven for approximately 18 minutes, or until it reaches an internal temperature of 120 degrees F. Allow the meat to rest approximately 5 minutes. Carve and serve with sauce.

Cabernet Mint Sauce -

Pick the mint leaves from the stem and place on cutting board. Sprinkle the sugar over the mint and chop together.

In a small sauce pot on medium heat, place the chopped mint and add the wine. Reduce by half the volume.

Add the demi-glacé and bring to a boil. Reduce heat and simmer and cook for 5 minutes.

Reduce heat to low and whisk in the butter. Season with salt and pepper.

Pulehu Lamb Chops

Serves 4

8	each	Double Lamb Chops
1	Tbsp	Garlic
1	Tbsp	*Alae* Salt
1	tsp	Cracked Pepper
1/4 tsp		Rosemary (freshly chopped)
1/4 tsp		Thyme (freshly chopped)
1/2 cup		Olive Oil

Marinade -

Mix all ingredients together, except for the lamb chops. Let marinade rest for 15 minutes before adding the lamb chops to marinade. Toss lamb chops and let marinade for 6 hours in the refrigerator.

Grill over mesquite or charcoal until desired doneness.

Pan Fried Ulua

lime butter sauce; green papaya and shrimp relish

Serves 4

4	each	Ulua Filets (6 oz. each)
1/4	cup	All Purpose Flour
4	Tbsp	Peanut Oil

Green Papaya and Shrimp Relish -

1/2	cup	Green Papaya (peeled, grated into match sticks)
1/8	cup	Bell Pepper (julienne)
1/8	cup	Red Onion (julienne)
1/4	cup	Bay Shrimp
1/8	tsp	*Ginger* (grated)
1/4	cup	Sugar
1/4	cup	Rice Wine Vinegar
		Patis to taste
		Salt & Pepper to taste

Lime Butter Sauce -

1/4	cup	Rice Wine Vinegar
1/4	cup	White Wine
1/8	cup	*Soy Sauce*
1	tsp	*Green Onions* (chopped)
1/4	cup	Heavy Cream
1/2	cup	Butter (cut into pieces)
3	each	Lime (juice and *zest*)

Green Papaya and Shrimp Relish -

Combine papaya, bell pepper, onion and *ginger* in a large bowl. Set aside until needed. In another bowl, add sugar, rice wine vinegar and *patis* (*fish sauce*) and stir until sugar dissolves. Toss vinegar mixture with the green papaya. Season with salt and pepper. Add bay shrimp and mix.

Lime Butter Sauce -

In a sauce pot, simmer lime juice, rice wine vinegar, *green onions*, white wine, lime *zest* and *soy sauce*. Reduce by half and add cream. Reduce again by half until cream thickens. Remove from heat and slowly add butter whisking constantly until smooth. Strain through a fine sieve and add lime *zest*. Season with salt and pepper.

Fish (ulua) -

Season fish with salt and pepper. Dredge in flour and sauté with in a hot pan with peanut oil. Sear one side until brown and turn to brown other side until fish is done.

To serve -

Place fish on plate, add Lime Butter Sauce and top with Green Papaya and Shrimp Relish.

In Hawai'i, some people always ask for ketchup -
ketchup this, ketchup that. So when I did the pulehu
lamb with a pineapple chutney salsa, I made a sauce for
local people using ketchup, Lea & Perrins. a little bit of
tabasco and brown sauce - it really went well together.
No, I don't get offended when people dump ketchup
over everything. I have friends who do it.
Hey, I do it myself...

Sweet Ending

Apple Crisp

Serves 8

Apple Mixture -

12	each	Apples (peeled and diced 1 inch)
1	cup	Sugar
1/3	cup	All Purpose Flour
1	Tbsp	Butter
		Cinnamon (to taste)

Crumb Topping -

1-1/2	cup	Butter (cold)
1-1/2	cup	Sugar
3	cup	All Purpose Flour
1/2	cup	Oatmeal

Method -

Mix crumb topping ingredients until crumbly (small balls). Make sure that you do not over mix.

Combine apple mixture ingredients in a bowl and set aside.

Butter the bottom of an 8 x 8 inch pan. Add apple mixture and top with crumb topping.

Bake in a pre-heated oven at 350 degrees F. for about 35 to 45 minutes or until mixture starts bubbling. Remove. Serve warm.

Baked Apple Tart

Serves 6

3	each	Granny Smith Apples
6	each	5 inch Puff Pastry Rounds
6	Tbsp	Sugar
1	tsp	Cinnamon
5	Tbsp	Butter (unsalted)

Method -

Peel apples, cut in half and remove seeds. Slice apples thinly trying to keep slices in place.

Layer apple slices on top of the puff pastry rounds. Sprinkle 1 tablespoon sugar and 1 teaspoon cinnamon. Dot with butter. Place on a sheet pan lined with baking or parchment paper. Repeat five more times. Bake in pre-heated oven for about 10 minutes at 375 degrees F. When pastry is golden brown, remove from oven. Serve immediately with whipped cream, vanilla ice cream or caramel mousse.

Double Lime Tart

One 9-inch tart

Crust -

1/4 cup	Unsalted Butter
1/8 cup	Brown Sugar
1 cup	All Purpose Flour
1/4 cup	Macadamia Nuts

Lime Cream -

1-1/2 cups	Sugar
1/3 cup	Cornstarch
2 cups	Water
3 each	Egg Yolks
2 Tbsp	Butter
1 Tbsp	Lime (*zest*)
1/3 cup	Lime (juice)

Lime Mousse -

4	Egg Yolks
1/2 cup	Sugar
1/3 cup	Lime (juice)
2 Tbsp	Gelatin
1/4 cup	Water
1 Tbsp	Lime (*zest*)
2 cups	Heavy Cream

Crust -

In a medium mixing bowl, combine all ingredients until crumbly (small balls). Remove and press into a 9-inch spring form pan. Bake in pre-heated oven at 350 degrees F. for 12 to 15 minutes or until golden brown. Cool.

Lime Cream -

In a medium *non-reactive pot*, cook the sugar, cornstarch and water over medium high heat until the cornstarch taste is eliminated. Temper the yolks by whisking them in a small bowl with a small amount of the sugar cornstarch mixture. Whisk the yolk into the pot, return to the heat, and continue to cook for 3 to 4 minutes. Add the butter, *zest* and juice and pour over the baked crust.

Lime Mousse -

Cook the yolks, sugar and lime juice over a double boiler until thick. Dissolve the gelatin in the water and add to the egg mixture. Add the lime *zest*. Cool. Whip the cream to soft peaks and fold into the mixture. Pour in the pan over the lime cream. Refrigerate for 4 to 6 hours then serve.

We used to have a starfruit tree in our backyard. We could eat 15 to 20 a day. We grew up surrounded by tropical fruits, like dragon eye, lychee, mountain apples, mangoes and avocado. To me, these fruits are not exotic. Growing up in Hawaii, "exotic" meant something like honeydew melon - stuff we could only get in a market.

Strawberry Tart

One 9-inch tart

Tart Dough -

1/2 cup	Sugar
1 cup	Butter
1 each	Egg
3 cups	All Purpose Flour
Dash	Salt
	Vanilla

Chocolate Ganache -

2 Tbsp	Heavy Cream
1/3 cup	Chocolate Chips

Pastry Cream -

2 cups	Milk
1/2 cup	Sugar
1/4 cup	Cornstarch
3 each	Egg Yolks
1 Tbsp	Butter
	Vanilla (to taste)
15 each	Strawberries (large)
1/2 cup	Apricot Glaze

Tart Dough -

In a mixing bowl, combine all ingredients except flour and mix. Add flour and mix until crumbly (small balls).

Roll dough 1 inch larger than your tart pan. Form into pan, trim sides. Poke holes with fork on bottom of tart dough.

Bake tart shells in oven 325 degrees F. for 15 to 25 minutes until golden brown. Cool.

Chocolate Ganache -

Heat the cream and add the chocolate chips and whisk until smooth. Set aside in a warm area until needed.

Pastry Cream -

In a stainless steel pot, add milk, sugar, cornstarch and egg yolks and cook slowly over low heat until the cornstarch taste is eliminated. Add butter and vanilla extract to taste.

Assembly of Fruit Tart -

Brush tart with chocolate ganache.

Pour pastry cream into crust to the top of the crust. Cool.

Place strawberries on top. Glaze with apricot glaze and refrigerate to set.

Baked Lemon Tart

One 9-inch tart

Crust -

1/2 cup	Butter
1/4 cup	Powdered Sugar
1	tsp	Lemon (*zest*)
1	cup	All Purpose Flour
		Pinch of Salt

Filling -

2	each	Eggs
1	cup	Sugar
3	Tbsp	All Purpose Flour
3	Tbsp	Lemon (juice)
1	tsp	Lemon (*zest*)
		Powdered Sugar for dusting

Crust -

Cream together butter and powdered sugar in a mixing bowl using a paddle. Add the lemon *zest*, flour and pinch of salt. Mix until smooth.

Press into tart shell or 9 x 9 inch cake pan. Bake in pre-heated oven at 350 degrees F. until golden brown (approximately 12 minutes). Remove.

Filling -

Whip together all the ingredients until smooth. Pour mixture into pan with the 9 inch baked crust or tart shell and bake it in a pre-heated oven at 350 degrees F. for 20 to 25 minutes. Remove and let set before slicing. Dust with powdered sugar before serving.

Lace Cookies

12 large cookies

1/2 cup	Butter	
1/2 cup	Light Corn Syrup	
3/4 cup	Brown Sugar (lightly packed)	
1 cup	All Purpose Flour (sifted)	
1-1/3 cup	*Macadamia Nuts* (chopped)	

Cook butter and corn syrup until butter is completely melted.

Combine the rest of the ingredients then add to butter mixture.

Grease pan well. Drop cookies and flatten a little. Bake in a pre-heated oven at 300 degrees F. in a oven for 8 to 10 minutes.

Chocolate Decadence

One 9-inch round cake

Method -

1 lb	Semi-sweet Chocolate Chips	
5 oz.	Butter	
5 each	Eggs	
1 Tbsp	All Purpose Flour	
1 Tbsp	Sugar	

Whip eggs until fluffy. Mix in flour and sugar until smooth. Reserve on side.

In a double boiler, melt chocolate with butter. Stir occasionally until chocolate is smooth. Fold chocolate mixture into egg batter. Pour batter into cake pan lined with parchment paper.

Bake for 25 minutes at 350 degrees F. Remove and cool. Chill before serving

Double Chocolate Mousse

Serves 12

Flourless Chocolate Cake (bottom half) -

1	cup	Bittersweet Chocolate
3-1/2	oz.	Butter
5	each	Egg Yolks
2-1/2	oz.	Sugar
5	each	Egg Whites
2-1/2	oz.	Sugar

Chocolate Mousse (top half) -

9	oz.	Bittersweet Chocolate
1/2	cup	Heavy Cream
3	each	Egg Yolks
3	Tbsp	Sugar
3	Tbsp	Butter (soften at room temperature)
1-1/2	cup	Heavy Cream

Flourless Chocolate Cake (bottom half) -

Line a 9-inch spring form pan with baking paper.

Melt the chocolate and butter over a double boiler. Whip the yolks and 2-1/2 ounces sugar until thick soft peaks appear. Fold in the chocolate mixture. Whip the whites and 2-1/2 ounces sugar creating soft peaks. Fold into chocolate mixture. Pour combined mixture into lined spring form pan and bake in preheated oven at 275 degrees F. for 1 hour. Cool.

Chocolate Mousse (top half) -

Melt the chocolate and 1/2 cup cream over double boiler. Whip the yolks and sugar until thick soft peaks appear. Add into the chocolate mixture. Add in the softened butter. Whip the 1-1/2 cups cream until soft peaks form and fold into mixture. Pour over the bottom half of the cake and chill for at least 6 hours.

To remove from pan, loosen the edges with a hot knife and remove the form.

Chocolate Semi Freddo

Serves 6

5	oz.	Bittersweet Chocolate
1/4	cup	Water
5/8	cup	Sugar
6	each	Egg Yolks
1-1/2	cup	Heavy Cream

Method -

In a double boiler, melt chocolate in a stainless steel bowl. In a sauce pot, boil together sugar and water until soft boil stage (120 degrees F.) In another mixing bowl, whip egg yolks until light and fluffy. Slowly whip in melted chocolate. Add boiled sugar and water gradually, whipping constantly. In another cold mixing bowl, whip heavy cream until a soft peak forms and fold into chocolate mixture. Pour into individual molds and freeze. Serve frozen.

Gingered Chocolate Pot de Creme

Serves 4 to 6

5	each	Egg Yolks
5	Tbsp	Sugar
1-1/2	tsp	Vanilla
2	cups	Heavy Cream
1/2	cup	Unsweetened Chocolate
1/4	cup	Semi Sweet Chocolate
1	tsp	Grated *Ginger*

Method -

Preheat oven to 350 degrees F.

In a stainless steel bowl, combine egg yolks, ginger, sugar and vanilla. Beat until light and fluffy. In another pot, add cream and chocolate and heat until chocolate melts. (Note: do not boil.)

Ladle hot cream into mixture, stirring constantly.

Strain custard through a sieve and portion into custard cups.

Place cups in a water bath, making sure the level of the water reaches at least halfway up the cup. Bake for at least 25 minutes, or until they are just cooked through. Do not overbake. Remove from water and cool. Serve cold with a dash of whipped cream, if desired.

Pumpkin Praline Pie

One 9-inch pie

Pie -

1	9-inch	Unbaked Pie Shell
2	each	Eggs
3/4	cup	Sugar
1/2	tsp	Salt
1	tsp	Cinnamon
1/2	tsp	*Ginger*
2	cups	Pumpkin Pie Filling
1-2/3	cups	Evaporated Milk

Praline Topping -

1/3	cup	Sugar
1/3	cup	Brown Sugar
3	Tbsp	Half and Half Cream
1/2	cup	Chopped Pecans

Pumpkin -

Mix all ingredients together and pour into 9-inch pie shell. Bake at 350 degrees F. for about 30 minutes or until center of pie is set.

Praline Topping -

Mix all ingredients together. Remove pumpkin pie from oven before it is almost done and top pie with mixture. Return pie into the oven for approximately 10 more minutes.

Bananas Foster

Serves 4

2	each	Bananas (quartered)
1	cup	Brown Sugar
3/4	cup	Butter
1	tsp	Cinnamon
1	each	Lemon (juice)
2	Tbsp	Creme 'de Banana
2	Tbsp	Rum (151 proof)
4	scoops	Vanilla Ice Cream

Method -

In a sauté pan, add brown sugar and butter. Simmer until smooth. Add cinnamon and lemon juice. Mix until smooth.

Add bananas and Creme 'de Banana. Simmer for 1 minute (until sugar mixture bubbles). Add rum and let alcohol dissipate.

To serve -

Serve over vanilla ice cream.

"3660" Chocolate Souffle Cake

Serves 20

Method -

2	lbs.	Bitter Sweet Chocolate
1	cup	Sweet Butter
16	each	Egg Yolks
1	cup	Sugar (granulated)
12	each	Egg Whites
1/2	cup	Sugar
		Vanilla Ice Cream
		Mocha or Chocolate Sauce to top

Melt chocolate and butter over double boiler.

Whip yolks and 1 cup sugar together until a ribbon forms. Do not over whip.

Fold chocolate into egg yolk mixture.

Whip egg whites with 1/2 cup sugar and fold into chocolate yolk mixture.

Portion batter into 20-6 oz. souffle cups. (Spray cups with pan grease then line bottom with parchment paper.)

Bake in an oven for 17 minutes at 325 degrees F.

Remove and serve immediately with vanilla ice cream and mocha or chocolate sauce.

*My mom taught me that you have to be organized when you bake. Baking is a precise science-
every ingredient has a purpose . . .
Baking isn't hard . . . but you have to like it.*

Banana Crisp with a Butter Pecan Topping

Serves 4

Banana Filling -

8	each	Bananas (sliced)
1	cup	Brown Sugar
2	Tbsp	Creme 'de Banana
2	Tbsp	Rum
1	each	Lemon (juice)
1/2	tsp	Cinnamon
3/4	cup	Butter

Crisp Topping -

1/2	cup	Unsalted Butter
1/2	cup	Light Brown Sugar
1	cup	All Purpose Flour
1/4	tsp	Salt
1/2	cup	Pecans
1	Tbsp	Granulated Sugar

Topping -
4   scoops Vanilla ice Cream

Crisp Topping -

Pre-heat oven to 350 degrees F.

In a bowl, cream 1/2 cup unsalted butter until light. Add the 1/2 cup brown sugar and granulated sugar gradually, mixing well after each addition leaving no lumps. Add flour and salt gradually to the mixture and mix until smooth. Stir in pecans.

Press into sheet pan and roll with a rolling pin until evenly distributed. Bake in oven for 35 minutes or until lightly golden and cooked through. Let cool. Break up cookie into small pieces.

Banana Filling -

In a skillet, add brown sugar and butter. Heat slowly until butter and sugar caramelizes. Add cinnamon, lemon juice and stir until smooth. Add Creme 'de Banana and rum and let simmer until alcohol dissipates. Add sliced bananas and cook for about 2 minutes.

To serve -

Place some of the cookie bits in the bottom of four bowls and put 1 scoop of vanilla ice cream in each. Top with banana mixture and cover with the balance of cookies.

Creme Caramel

Serves 8

3/4 cup	Sugar
1/4 cup	Water
3 each	Eggs
1 each	Egg Yolk
1-1/2 cup	Milk
1/2 cup	Whipping Cream
1/2 Tbsp	Vanilla Extract
3/8 cup	Sugar

Caramel -

To make the caramel, add 3/4 cup sugar and 1/4 cup water in a medium thickness sauce pot. Cook over medium heat, stirring once or twice to dissolve the sugar. Let mixture bubble slowly until it turns golden brown. Remove from heat immediately and pour caramel into a flan mold.

In a stainless steel bowl, combine the eggs, egg yolk and 3/8 cup sugar. Mix until smooth. Slowly stir in the milk and whipping cream being careful not to froth the mixture too much. Add vanilla extract and stir. Pour mixture into flan mold with caramel mixture. Place mold in a water bath, making sure water level is half that of the mold. Bake in pre-heated oven at 325 degrees F. for about 1 hour and 30 minutes. Insert knife into middle of the custard. If it comes out smoothly, the custard is done. Remove mold and let set at room temperature for about 1 hour. Refrigerate for about 2 to 3 hours.

Remove from mold by sliding knife along the edge of the mold. Invert and pour remaining caramel over custard. Most of the solid caramel will remain in mold.

This is liliko'i all the way and it's very Hawai'i. . .
We use it in its natural state and incorporate it with the
cheesecake. I don't use any compounds, just the natural
juices. . . Liliko'i is so unique with a beautiful flavor,
you don't want to ruin it. . .

Liliko'i Cheesecake

Serves 12

Crust -

1/2 cup	Butter
1/4 cup	Brown Sugar
1/2 cup	Macadamia Nuts (chopped)
1 cup	All Purpose Flour

Cheesecake -

2 cups	Cream Cheese
1/2 cup	Sugar
5 each	Egg Yolks
1/2 cup	Sugar
1/4 cup	Water
1 Tbsp	Gelatin
1/4 cup	Liliko'i Purée (passion fruit)
1-1/2 cup	Heavy Cream (whipped)

Topping -

1 cup	Clear Gel (agar agar)
1/3 cup	*Liliko'i* Purée

Crust -

Prepare 9-inch spring form (cake) pan lined with paper. Mix butter, sugar and nuts. Add flour and mix. Do not overmix. Mixture should be crumbly. Press into pan, 1/4 up the side. Bake in pre-heated oven at 350 degrees F. for 10 to 12 minutes.

Cheesecake -

Cream together cream cheese and 1/2 cup sugar. Mix egg yolks and 1/2 cup sugar and cook over double boiler. When egg mixture is thick, take off heat and set aside until needed. In a small cup, dissolve gelatin in water. Add gelatin to egg mixture making sure gelatin dissolves well. Add liliko'i purée and mix together. Add the egg mixture to the cream cheese mix. Fold in whipped cream. Pour into crust and refrigerate for about 5 hours.

Melt 1 cup clear gelatin and mix in 1/3 cup liliko'i purée. Spread over the chilled cake.

Pear Upside-Down Cake

One 9-inch cake- serves 12

Cake Batter -

2-1/2 cup	Flour
1-1/2 tsp	Baking Soda
1 tsp	Ground Cinnamon
1 tsp	Ground *Ginger*
1/4 tsp	Ground Cloves
1 tsp	Salt
1/2 cup	Molasses
1/2 cup	Honey
3/4 cup	Hot Water
1 each	Egg
1/2 cup	Sugar
8 Tbsp	Unsalted Butter (softened)
1/4 cup	Butter
1/2 cup	Light Brown Sugar
2 Tbsp	Dark Rum

Pears -

5 each	Fresh Pears (peeled)
4 cups	Water
1 tsp	Vanilla
1 each	Lemon (juice)
1 cup	Sugar

Cake Batter -

In a mixing bowl, sift dry ingredients.
Set aside.

Combine molasses, honey and water.
Set aside.

Beat 1 egg and 1/2 cup sugar until creamy. Add 8 tablespoons softened butter and mix. To butter mixture, add small amounts of wet and dry ingredients alternately until done.

Grease 9-inch pan and line bottom with baking paper.

Melt together in a sauce pan:
1/4 cup butter, 1/2 cup light brown sugar (packed), and 2 tablespoons dark rum.

Pour mixture into prepared baking pan. Fan pears (see below) around bottom of pan.
Pour cake batter over pears. Bake 40 to 45 minutes in a pre-heated oven at 350 degrees F. Cool and turn out cake.

To prepare pears -

In a medium sauce pot, combine all ingredients except pears. Heat mixture to boil then turn down to a simmer. Add pears. Poach pears until tender. Remove from poaching liquid and cool. Cool liquid and store pears in liquid until ready to use.

Liliko'i Mousse

Serves 8

1/3 cup	Liliko'i Purée (passion fruit)	
1	cup	Sugar
8	Tbsp	Butter
4	each	Eggs
1	tsp	Gelatin (plain)
1/4 cup	Water	
1/2 cup	Mascarpone Cheese	
2	Tbsp	Heavy Cream

plus another -

3/4 cup	Heavy Cream

Method -

Cook *liliko'i* purée, sugar and butter until butter is melted. Set aside.

Beat eggs until frothy, then add *liliko'i* mixture. Return to stove and cook over low heat until thick.

Dissolve gelatin with water. Add to above mixture, stir and cool.

Mix cheese and 2 tablespoons heavy cream. Add the cooled *liliko'i* mixture, a little at a time.

Whip 3/4 cup heavy cream until soft peaks form. Fold into above mixture. Refrigerate.

155

Liliko'i Chiffon Pie

One 9 inch pie

7 each Egg Yolks

3/4 cup Sugar

3/4 cup *Liliko'i* Purée
(passion fruit)

3/4 cup Water

1-1/2 Tbsp Gelatin

3/4 cup Sugar

7 each Egg Whites

Whipped Cream
for topping

Method -

In a pot, add egg yolks, 3/4 cup sugar, and *liliko'i* fruit purée. Whip until smooth over low heat. When sauce starts to thicken, add gelatin (dissolve with 3/4 cup water) mixture. Mix until smooth. Set aside and cool to room temperature. Whip egg whites and add 3/4 cup sugar gradually to create soft peaks. Fold into *liliko'i* mixture. Pour into a 9-inch pre-baked pie shell. Chill.

To serve -

Top with whipped cream before serving.

Liliko'i Napoleon

liliko'i mousse

Serves 6

Liliko'i Mousse -

1/3 cup	Liliko'i Purée (passion fruit)
1	cup	Sugar
8	Tbsp	Butter
4	each	Eggs
2	tsp	Gelatin
1/4 cup	Water
1/2 cup	Mascarpone Cheese
3/4 cup	Heavy Cream

Filo Leaves -

5 leaves	Filo Pastry
1/3 lb	Butter (melted)
1/3 cup	Granulated Sugar

In a non-reactive pot, cook the butter, sugar and purée over medium heat until the butter is melted and the sugar is dissolved.

Whip the eggs in a mixing bowl. Add the butter mixture to the bowl and mix. Pour this mixture back into the pot and cook over low heat until it reaches a temperature of 160 degrees F; about 5 to 7 minutes. Dissolve the gelatin in the water and add to the mixture in the pot. Cool.

Place the mascarpone cheese in a large bowl and add the cooled mixture and gently fold in. Whip the cream to soft peaks and fold into the cheese mixture. Cool.

Filo Leaves -

Lay one sheet of filo on a clean, dry table or cutting board. Keep the unused sheets covered to prevent them from drying out. Brush the filo with a light coat of the melted butter. Sprinkle it with a light coat of sugar. Cover with a second pastry and repeat step number 2. Continue until you have used all the sheets. Brush top sheet lightly with butter.

With a pastry wheel (pizza cutter), cut into even squares, rectangles or triangles. Place a piece of parchment paper on an inverted baking tray. Transfer the pastry to the tray and cover with a second piece of parchment, then cover it with a second baking tray to form a sandwich. Bake in a preheated oven at 325 degree F. for 15 minutes.

To Assemble -

Scoop the mousse into a piping bag with a round tip. Pipe a small amount of the mousse onto the middle of the plate. Place one piece of the pastry on the plate and pipe the mouse following the dimensions of the pastry.

Place a second pastry on top of the mousse and pipe the mousse on the pastry, again following the shape of the pastry.

Top with a third rectangular or square of pastry and pipe a small rosette of the mousse and dust with powdered sugar. Garnish with a sprig of mint.

Texture is right up there with the others - you have to
have taste, good presentation... and texture - it's like my
triangle. When you eat Jello, it's one-dimensional, Jello
is Jello, but using the triangle, you make it three-dimen-
sional...you have a full-fledged sculpture. By having texture in your food, it prevents the monotony in eating,
especially after the first bite...it's like "3-D food."

Fresh Strawberry Napoleon

white chocolate mousse

Serves 8

9	oz.	White Chocolate (melted)
2-3/4	oz.	Egg Whites (whipped to soft peak)
1-1/4	oz.	Sugar
1	Tbsp	Water
24	each	Strawberries (large)

Cream -

2	cups	Heavy Cream

Method -

In a large sauce pot, cook sugar and water until it reaches a soft ball consistency. Remove and place it in a mixer. Set aside until needed. In another mixing bowl, whip egg whites to soft peaks. Add to sugar and water in the mixer on slow speed. After melting chocolate on a double boiler, add chocolate to mixture also on slow speed.

Cream -

Whip cream to soft peaks and fold into white chocolate mixture.

To serve -

Using your favorite shortbread cookie recipe, cut out eighteen 4 inch diameter circles. Bake until done.

On one cookie, pipe mousse to cover. Place sliced strawberries on top with cookie and repeat. Top with cookie and dust with powdered sugar, rosette of mousse and mint sprig.

Macadamia Nut Crepe with Strawberries

Serves 4

Crepes -

1/2 cup	Unsalted Macadamia Nuts (finely chopped)
1/2 cup	Flour
1/2 cup	Water
1/4 cup	Milk
2 each	Eggs (large)
1-1/2 Tbsp	Melted Butter, cooled
1/2 tsp	Vanilla Extract
1/2 tsp	Sugar
2 cup	Vanilla Ice Cream
	Pinch of Salt

Strawberry Sauce -

1 cup	Strawberry Sauce
1-1/2 cup	Strawberries (sliced) Reserve 1/2 cup
1/4 cup	Whipping Cream
4 sprigs	Mint Leaf
	Powder Sugar for Dusting

Crepes -

Mix macadamia nuts with flour in a mixing bowl. Add water, milk, eggs, vanilla, sugar and salt. Mix for a minute. Scrape sides and fold in the butter. Let batter rest for an hour before making crepes.

On each crepe, spoon on 1/4 cup of the vanilla ice cream. Top with sliced berries and roll up crepe. Repeat until 8 crepes are completed.

Strawberry Sauce -

Mix together strawberry sauce and the remaining 1/2 cup of strawberries. Ladle over crepes. Top with a spoonful of whipped cream, dust with the powder sugar and garnish with a sprig of mint.

Jasmine Rice Pudding

Serves 4

1/2 cup	Jasmine Rice
1	each	Vanilla Bean
2	cups	Milk
Pinch	Salt
1	cup	Whipping Cream
3/8 cup	Sugar
1/2 tsp	Gelatin

Method -

Bring rice, vanilla bean, milk and salt to a boil. Turn heat down and cover. Simmer over very low heat.

Cook until rice absorbs all the liquid. Stir every so often so rice will not burn. Add sugar after milk is completely absorbed by rice. Mix thoroughly.

Dissolve gelatin with a little water until smooth. Add to rice and stir.

Whip heavy cream until a soft peak forms and fold into rice mixture. Spoon mixture into molds and chill.

Unmold and sprinkle with sugar glaze under broiler until sugar carmelizes.

Serve with a berry coulis.

Final Thoughts

I believe that everyone should have their own cuisine. People should use what they know, incorporate what they like, test their own skills, and find their own niche. Every chef wants to make their mark. We have many artistic, talented young people today—many with very good palates. Those who are interested in cooking must go out and find their own path. They must give their tastes a chance to mature and blossom. Given that experience, their own style will eventually come through.

Personally, I know I'll never be wholly satisfied with the quality of my food. I'll always think I can be better. "You are your own competition—not the other restaurants in town," I tell my chefs. Regardless of what it is you do, you have to focus on improving yourself. You can't waste your time thinking about your competition. Look within yourself; push yourself to be better. Then it will come...

Acknowledgements

Gale Ogawa
Lisa Siu
Sunny & Cecilia Kim
Marlene, Nino & Victoria Murray
Audrey Muromoto
Dave Miyamoto
Bud Muth
Bob Funt

3660 On The Rise Restaurant Staff

Conversion Table

Liquid Measures

Fluid Ounces	U.S. Measures	Imperial Measures	Milliliters
	1 tsp	1 tsp	5
1/4	2 tsp	1 dessert spoon	7
1/2	1 Tbsp	1 Tbsp	15
1	2 Tbsp	2 Tbsp	28
2	1/4 cup	4 Tbsp	56
4	1/2 cup or 1/4 pint		110
5		1/4 pint or 1 gill	140
6	3/4 cup		170
8	1 cup or 1/2 pint		225
9			250 or 1/4 liter
10	1-1/4 cups	1/2 pint	280
12	1-1/2 cups or 3/4 pint		240
15		3/4 pint	420
16	2 cups or 1 pint		450
18	2-1/4 cups		500 or 1/2 liter
20	2-1/2 cups	1 pint	560
24	3 cups or 1-1/2 pints		675
25		1-1/4 pints	700
27	3-1/2 cups		750
30	3-3/4 cups	1-1/2 pints	840
32	4 cups or 2 pints or 1 quart		900
35		1-1/4 pints	980
36	4-1/2 cups		1000 or 1 liter

Solid Measures

Ounces	Pounds	Grams	Kilos
1		28	
2		56	
3-1/2		100	
4	1/4	112	
5		140	
6		168	
8	1/2	225	
9		250	1/4
12	3/4	340	
16	1	450	
18		500	1/2
20	1-1/4	560	
24	1-1/2	675	
27		750	3/4
28	1-3/4	780	
32	2	900	
36	2-1/4	1000	1
40	2-1/2	1100	
48	3	1350	
54		1500	1-1/2

Oven Temperature Equivalents

Fahrenheit	Gas Mark	Celsius	Heat of Oven
225	1/4	107	Very Cool
250	1/2	121	Very Cool
275	1	135	Cool
300	2	148	Cool
325	3	163	Moderate
350	4	177	Moderate
375	5	190	Fairly Hot
400	6	204	Fairly Hot
425	7	218	Hot
450	8	232	Very Hot
475	9	246	Very Hot

Glossary of Terms

'ahi: Hawaiian yellow-fin tuna

aioli: thick mayonnaise flavored with garlic

alae: Hawaiian word meaning a coarse, dark, reddish-brown colored sea salt

ama ebi: a sweet, deep water shrimp

bonito flakes: dried fish flakes, usually made from tuna

brown sauce: made from brown stock, brown roux, mirepoix, tomatoes and herbs

brunoise: vegetables, etc. that are diced very small

cake noodles: thin noodles, pan sautéed to a crispy texture on both sides, with the inside still moist and soft

carpaccio: raw beef or fish filets, sliced very thin; served with mustard sauce, or olive oil and lemon juice

chanterelle mushrooms: an orange-ish trumpet-shaped mushroom with ruffled edges

Chinese black bean sauce: preserved and fermented salty black beans

Chinese parsley: cilantro

confit: any meat or poultry cooked and preserved in its own fat; vegetables or fruits cooked and preserved in brandy or a liquor syrup

cumin: herb used in India, Mexico and the Middle East cuisine which gives chili its characteristic flavor

daikon: Japanese variety of a long, white radish, approximately a foot in length

dashi konbu: dried seaweed used for soup stock

demi glacé: basic brown sauce reduced with veal stock and flavored with sherry or madeira wine

fish sauce: salted, fermented fish made into a sauce or oil (patis)

five spice: fennel seeds, cinnamon, star anise, cloves, peppercorns and/or licorice root ground into a powder

galanga root: related to the ginger family, with a similar taste

green onion: spring onion, shallots

guava: tropical fruit with a thick, yellow skin and a pinkish pulp inside; used mostly for jams and jellies

hoisin: reddish, slightly sweet, bean sauce, seasoned with garlic and chilis

katsu: meat, chicken or fish, dipped in egg and very fine bread crumbs (panko), then fried or deep-fried

kumquat: small, oblong fruit with a citrus taste; the rind is sweet, pulp is sour; also used for zest

laulau: Hawaiian term meaning "to wrap," or "a wrapped package"; wrapped in ti leaves or banana leaves; these usually contain pork, beef, salted fish, and taro leaves; traditionally baked in an underground oven, or imu

lemon grass: naturally lemon-scented, pampas-like grass; used mostly in Vietnamese and Thai food

liliko'i: passion fruit

lup cheong: Chinese sausage made with sweetened pork

lychee: reddish, round fruit with a tough outer skin; fresh pulp is translucent to pale white; very sweet flavor

macadamia nut: a whitish, sweet, round nut; sold already roasted, although it is also delicious eaten raw roux; a thickener for sauces made with butter, or fat and flour

mahimahi: sporty game fish, measuring up to 4 to 5 feet long

menlo paper: spring roll wrapper; similar to rice paper wrappers, except made with flour

mesclun: variety of mixed greens

mirepoix: diced vegetables, herbs and fat, for flavoring brown soups and sauces

mirin: light, sweet rice wine used for cooking

mochi: sweet rice cakes, made from a special, glutinous rice

mooshoo: pasta wrappers, similar to ravioli

musubi: lightly salted rice balls, often wrapped in nori (dried seaweed); some times stuffed with a condiment, ranging from salted pickled plums, to small pieces of fish or meat; not to be confused with sushi

Napoleon: dessert of puff pastry with pastry creme; stacked in layers

non-reactive pot: basically, pots and pans that are not made of aluminum

nori: dried seaweed; usually molded into thin sheets

ogo: seaweed, ranging in color from reddish-brown to dark green; grows close to shore in Hawaii, or commercially grown in aquaculture facilities; called manauea in Hawaiian

'Opakapaka: Pacific pink snapper

oyster sauce: thick, dark sauce made with oysters, salt and a variety of seasonings

pancetta: Italian version of cured bacon (not smoked), made with salt, pepper and spices

panko: fine bread crumbs

patis: fish sauce made with salted, fermented fish

plum sauce: Chinese sweet-sour sauce made from plums, apricots, sugar and vinegar

poi: pasty Hawaiian staple made by pounding cooked taro and mixing it with water

poke: sliced or cubed raw fish with various ingredients and seasonings

ponzu sauce: thick Japanese sauce with its own unique flavor; often used like a dipping sauce for cutlets; similar in use to worchestershire sauce

porcini mushroom: wild mushroom with a thick cap and stem

portobello mushroom: large, Italian wild mushroom

Portuguese sausage: spicy pork sausage

prosciutto: dry, air-cured ham; not smoked

pulehu: to char-broil meats, fish, poultry, vegetables or fruits

pupu: appetizer or hors d' oeuvres

quesadilla: thin tortilla, folded and often stuffed with cheese, then broiled

ricotta salata: hard, aged, ricotta cheese; shaved like parmesan cheese over salads

roulade: sliced meats rolled around a stuffing; browned, then braised slowly

saimin: noodle soup, often made with pork broth and garnished with small meat morsels and vegetables

shiitake: thick, dark brown mushroom with smooth, velvety caps on the outside; available either dried or fresh

shiso leaf: member of the mint family with a unique, peppery fresh flavor used fresh, dried or powdered

shrimp paste: salted fermented shrimp used for seasoning

soba: noodles made from buckwheat flour

somen: thin, round, white wheat noodles

soy sauce: slightly sweet and salty sauce made from wheat flour and fermented soybeans

star anise: star-shaped pod, very sweet and aromatic; used in many Asian dishes

sukiyaki: thinly sliced beef and a variety of vegetables cooked in a beef or pork broth seasoned with soy sauce

taro: Hawaiian staple, starchy in texture, like a potato; farmed in shallow running water ponds, or lo'i

teriyaki: means glazed and broiled; meat, fish, poultry, or vegetables that are marinated in a sweet and salty soy sauce mixture, then grilled or broiled

ti leaf: plant with shiny, purplish red or green leaves, about 15 to 20 inches long, and 4 to 6 inches wide; used in Hawaiian cooking to wrap or cover food

tobiko: flying fish roe

tofu: fresh bean curd cake; white with texture of well-baked custard

uku: deep sea snapper

ulua: white meat fish from the crevalle jack or pompano family

wasabi: green horseradish with a strong, biting, refreshing taste; used with raw seafood and sushi dishes

won ton pi: Chinese noodle wrapper similar to a pasta wrapper

zest: the outer rind of any citrus fruit, chopped very fine and used for flavoring

Cookbook Sponsors

Superior Coffee

Boyd's Coffee

Y. Fukunaga Products, Inc.

Lyle Hamasaki Construction, Inc.

Hawaii Plastics Corp.

Tropic Fish & Vegetable Center

The Pint Size Corporation

Index

172

Index

The Crew

From L to R: Geo Loyo, James Grant Benton, Arnold T. Hiura, Russell Siu,
Craig Uchimura, Ric Noyle, Lisa A. Kim & Jim Gillespie

Grant & Hiura was formed in 1992 out of a longtime friendship between Glen L. Grant and Arnold T. Hiura. They were joined by James Grant Benton in 1995. As individuals and as a creative team, the company has produced a variety of books, brochures, and scripts; consulted on marketing and public relations programs; and offered historical tours and programs; as well as provided an effective and entertaining method of corporate training utilizing humor and local culture.

Geo Loyo & Craig Uchimura designers from Kramer & Associates Design, a company that specializes in printed collateral, corporate identity and environmental graphic design for major resorts, restaurants and entertainment centers world-wide.

Ric Noyle whose taste-tempting photographs throughout *On the Rise* are testimony to his professional approach in presenting images which capture the essence of Russell's dishes.

Lisa A. Kim is the owner of L.A.K. Enterprises, which specializes in strategic marketing, public relations, event coordination and publishing. Since establishing her business five years ago, Lisa has built upon her already extensive background in Hawaii's visitor industry to include sales and marketing projects for a variety of private corporations, as well as coordination of events promoting the state of Hawaii around the world.

James M. Gillespie has been a resident chef at 3660 On the Rise since September 1992. Graduating from the Culinary Institute of America in 1982, James has travelled throughout the Western U.S., creating excellent cuisine at hotels and clubs such as the Externship Hotel Meridian in Houston, the Club Corporation of America, as well as various other clubs in Dallas, Los Angeles and San Francisco.